Constitu[tional Law]
Questions and Explanatory Answers for Law School and the Bar Exam

Volume II

Dr. Eric Engle LL.M.

Copyright © 2023 Eric Engle

All rights reserved.

DEDICATION

For my family

CONTENTS

Constitutional Law Quiz Questions and Explanatory Answers for
Law School and the Bar Exam...i

Constitutional Law Quiz Questions and Explanatory Answers for
Law School and the Bar Exam..1

Introduction..1

Give the holding in Marbury v. Madison..3

Give the holding in McCulloch v. Maryland......................................5

We just saw Marshall "tag team" the States with the elastic clause
and the supremacy clause. Can you briefly restate those two basic
constitutional rules?..7

Are State and Federal powers respectively mutually exclusive or can
there be concurrent federal and state power?.....................................8

Name the express exclusive federal powers.......................................9

Are there any exclusively state powers? If so, name them...............10

What is the first or most important case to extend federal power by a
"tag team" of the commerce clause and the elastic clause ("necessary
and proper")?...11

What is the establishment clause? What is the general test for
determining whether a law violates the establishment clause of the
First Amendment?..14

Who bears the burden of proof that there is a "rational basis" linking
the means chosen by government and some permissible end of
governance, the government or the person claiming a government act
is unconstitutional?..17

Who bears the burden of proof when reviewing a law against the
constitution and applying intermediate or strict scrutiny?...............18

What are the three main categories of laws that are subject to rational basis review?...19

To which categories does intermediate scrutiny apply?...................21

What burden does the strict scrutiny standard impose?...................23

What is the presumption associated with strict scrutiny when it is applied to a law?...25

Which suspect classes are protected by strict scrutiny review?.......27

What is "Commercial Speech"?..28

Are states permitted to pass laws that limit commercial speech?....29

Is commercial speech subject to strict scrutiny, intermediate scrutiny, or rational review (means-ends) review?...........................30

What are the two primary factors considered when determining the constitutionality of restrictions on commercial speech?...................32

What requirements must be met by a law that limits commercial speech if the speech is neither misleading nor illegal?.....................34

What is the purpose of the equal protection clause? How does it function?...35

What is the standard of review applied when equal protection is at issue?..37

What is the standard of review used when determining the constitutionality of a law under the equal protection clause?...........39

What are the requirements that must be met by laws limiting speech in a private forum and a limited public forum?...............................40

What are the requirements that must be satisfied by laws that restrict speech in a public forum?...43

What is the State action requirement in relation to the protection of freedom of speech?...45

What is the jurisdiction of the Supreme Court of the United States?

What types of cases may it hear?..47

Is Congress authorized to appoint officials for the purpose of enforcing acts of Congress?..50

What is meant by the term "inferior officer"?..................................52

Who has the constitutional authority to appoint inferior officers of the United States?...54

What is procedural due process?..55

What factors are taken into account during a procedural due process analysis?...56

What are the two primary powers granted to the federal government under the commerce clause?...57

What is the extent of the president's foreign affairs power under Article II?...59

What methods can the federal government employ to require a state to enact a particular legislative action?...60

Is it permissible for a private citizen to file a lawsuit against a state? 61

What role does the Eleventh Amendment play in private citizens suing a state?...62

Name some of the most important recent Indian law Supreme Court cases..63

Under what circumstances can a citizen sue a state government?...65

Is the power to regulate interstate commerce exclusively federal or instead is it a concurrent state and federal power or is it instead a power of the several states, only?..66

What is meant by the term "dormant commerce clause"?...............68

Under what circumstances does a state law violate the dormant commerce clause?...70

In what two ways can a law violate the commerce clause?.............72

What is the balancing test used to evaluate the dormant commerce clause?...74

When is the dormant commerce clause balancing test applied?......74

What is the standard of review for controversies involving aliens as a class?...76

Is it permissible for a private citizen to sue a state in federal court? 77

Can a member of a sovereign Native American tribe sue a state in federal court?...78

Can the state of New York sue the state of California in federal court?..80

Is it permissible for a foreign government to sue a U.S. state in federal court?...81

Does the U.S. President have the authority to decline to spend funds that were appropriated by Congress for a particular purpose?..........82

What types of laws may be passed under the 13th Amendment?....84

Under what circumstances does a government worker have a property right in their position?..86

If a government worker has a property right in their position, what must they be afforded before termination?.....................................88

What are the requirements for regulating commercial speech?.......90

What is obscenity?...93

Is a state government permitted to impose restrictions on obscenity? 95

If a treaty between the United States and another country conflicts with a state law, is the U.S. President authorized to declare the state law invalid?...96

Define: substantive due process..98

What does procedural due process guarantee?..............................100

What does substantive due process guarantee?..............................102

From which constitutional clause is substantive due process protection derived? Include, if possible, specific text quoted from the relevant provisions of the U.S. Constitution....................................104

Name some landmark cases that shaped substantive due process. 105

What are some examples of fundamental rights?...........................107

What is the limit on Congress's power to investigate and subpoena? 109

What conditions must be present for Congress to properly regulate state action through the spending power? That is, when and how may congress condition grants of funds to states?..................................111

May a state tax a publication based on its content?.......................114

What is the constitutional limit on public school punishments?....116

Would prohibiting religious groups from meeting on school property violate the Constitution?..118

When Do citizens have standing to sue the federal or state government, to compel it to act constitutionally?............................120

When may a citizen sue the government to act constitutionally?. .122

Define: Preemption...124

Preemption: What factors are considered when determining whether federal law preempts a state law?..126

Does the presence of a provision within a state law that attempts to resolve conflicts with federal law affect the determination of whether the state law is preempted by federal law?.....................................128

What happens if the Supreme Court of the United States (SCOTUS) is deciding on a state court ruling and there is a split decision, with a 50% versus 50% outcome?..129

Discuss the most important cases on preemption law....................130

Is it permissible for a state to require a federal worker, who is driving through the state on federal business, to possess a valid state driver's license?...132

If a local town library is sued for purportedly violating a federal law, can it claim sovereign immunity?...133

Is it constitutional for a homeowners association (HOA) to pass a rule prohibiting residents from raising the American flag on the 4th of July?...134

Give the Holding in Shelly v. Kramer...136

Define: bill of attainder?..138

When a ratified treaty conflicts with an act of Congress, which one takes precedence? Is the rule the same for unratified treaties?.......140

What is the definition of an at-large election?...............................142

Under what circumstances is an at-large election considered unconstitutional?..143

What is the purpose of the equal protection clause in the Constitution, and how does it safeguard against discriminatory treatment by state governments?...145

Under what circumstances does private action qualify as state action, triggering the application of constitutional protections such as the equal protection clause?...146

Answer: Can you provide an example of private action in which the government's involvement is not significant enough to be considered state action, thus exempting it from constitutional scrutiny?..........147

Some Final Exam Tips!...149

CONCLUSION..151

ACKNOWLEDGMENTS

I want to thank the Flower Memorial Library for having made this book possible.

Constitutional Law Quiz Questions and Explanatory Answers for Law School and the Bar Exam

Volume II

Dr. Eric Engle LL.M.

Introduction

Are you ready to embark on an exciting journey towards mastering constitutional law? You're in the right place! *Constitutional Law Quiz Questions and Explanatory Answers for Law School and the Bar Exam* is here to ignite your passion for the constitutional law and equip you with the tools for success.

As a law student or a bar prep candidate, you understand the importance of a solid foundation in constitutional law. This comprehensive book is carefully crafted to cater to your unique needs, providing you with a dynamic learning experience like no other.

Inside these pages you'll discover a treasure trove of engaging quiz questions designed to challenge your understanding of key concepts, landmark cases, and constitutional principles. But that's not all – accompanying each question are detailed explanatory answers that will unravel the intricacies of the law, empowering you with a deep comprehension of its application, including summaries of leading cases and memory methods such as acronyms, mnemonics, and bold imagery.

All that makes this book more than just a collection of quiz questions and answers – it's a roadmap to success in law school exams and the bar exam. Alongside the quiz questions, you'll find valuable study tips, exam preparation strategies, and test-taking techniques that have been honed by seasoned legal professionals. These insights will help you navigate through constitutional law complexes with confidence, precision, and passion.

Whether you're a law school student striving for top grades or a bar exam candidate aiming to conquer the final hurdle, "Constitutional Law Quiz Questions and Explanatory Answers for Law School and the Bar Exam" is your ultimate companion. It will sharpen your legal analysis skills, enhance your critical thinking abilities, and deepen your understanding of constitutional law.

So, jump right into the world of constitutional law with enthusiasm and determination. Let this book be your guide, your study partner, and your trusted resource. Prepare to go beyond mere memorization to truly grasp the underlying principles that shape our legal system. Don't just study – immerse yourself in the dynamic realm of constitutional law. When you understand *why* the law is it is much easier to remember what the law *is* and to better argue on exams and briefs. Equip yourself with the knowledge to gain expertise and confidence so you excel in law school and the bar exam. Embrace this engaging opportunity to trigger your curiousity and become a constitutional law champ!

Are you ready? Unlock your true potential in the fascinating world of constitutional law. The journey begins now!

Give the holding in Marbury v. Madison

Marbury held: ordinary legislation can be reviewed against the constitution. If there is a conflict between ordinary legislation and the constitution the ordinary legislation must be held unenforceable, void, as unconstitutional.

Facts: Conflict between the appointments made by outgoing President John Adams and incoming President Thomas Jefferson. Were signed, and sealed, but not delivered. Plaintiff sought mandamus to compel delivery. Held: Marbury, one of the appointees, was entitled to his commission, but the provision of the Judiciary Act of 1789, which Marbury relied upon to seek his commission, was unconstitutional as arrogating jurisdiction beyond that expressed in the constitution. Supreme Court has the authority to interpret the Constitution and strike down laws that are inconsistent with it. "It is emphatically the province and duty of the judicial department to say what the law is." Marshall, CJ.

Judicial review is found in the Federalist Papers. Federalist No. 78:

"Whoever attentively considers the different departments of power must perceive that, in a government in which they are separated from each other, the judiciary, from the nature of its functions, will always be the least dangerous to the political rights of the Constitution; because it will be least in a capacity to annoy or injure them. The Executive not only dispenses the honors, but holds the sword of the community. The legislature not only commands the purse, but prescribes the rules by which the duties and rights of every citizen are to be regulated. The judiciary, on the contrary, has no influence over either the sword or the purse; no direction either of the strength or of the wealth of the society; and can take no active resolution whatever. It may truly be said to have neither FORCE nor WILL, but merely judgment; and must ultimately depend upon the aid of the executive arm even for the efficacy of its judgments." (Federalist No.

78). Likewise, the implication federal power necessary and proper to implement express aims and powers of the federation can be found in the Federalist Papers, Federalist No. 33 where Hamilton discusses the necessary and proper clause: "It may be affirmed with perfect confidence that the constitutional operation of the intended government would be precisely the same, if these clauses [the necessary and proper clause] were entirely obliterated, as if they were repeated in every article. They are only declaratory of a truth which would have resulted by necessary and unavoidable implication from the very act of constituting a federal government, and vesting it with certain specified powers." (Federalist No. 33). Article I, Section 8, Clause 18 of the United States Constitution.

Memory tricks:

Here are some fun limericks. You should ENJOY the study of law, whether by quizzing your friends with these quiz books, writing up your own poems or lyrics, searching through cases for earlier or parallel authority. Make law school fun because the most effective learning environments are enjoyable and safe. People don't perform well under pressure and threat or when bored. Try to relate whatever you study in law to your own experiences, goals, and beliefs, then it takes on relevance and becomes more memorable!

Marbury's commission, lost in transition,
Madison's refusal, sparked a legal mission.
Justice Marshall, with wisdom and grace,
Established judicial review, putting power in its place.

*

A midnight judge, caught in a political game,
Marbury's hopes, hung by a constitutional frame.
Marshall's holding, a stroke of judicial might,
"Marbury's right, but mandamus denied," he recites.

Give the holding in McCulloch v. Maryland

McCulloch held: the Court can imply all necessary and proper powers (means) to the ends of the the express powers of the constitution (ends). Established the principle of judicial review. Supreme Court has power to declare acts of Congress unconstitutional if they violated the Constitution.

McCulloch v. Maryland, 1819: Second Bank of the United States. Maryland had imposed a tax on the 2d US bank. Issue: whether the state. Held: Congress had the power to establish a national bank under the Necessary and Proper Clause of the Constitution. This clause, also known as the Elastic Clause, grants Congress the authority to enact laws that are necessary and proper to carry out its enumerated powers; broad interpretation of federal powers and federal government has implied powers beyond those explicitly listed in the Constitution: "Let the end be legitimate, let it be within the scope of the Constitution, and all means which are appropriate, which are plainly adapted to that end, which are not prohibited, but consist with the letter and spirit of the Constitution, are constitutional." Marshall, CJ. This appears to be the judicial origin of means-ends rational review. The means must be reasonable the end legitimate.

McCulloch v. Maryland expanded scope of federal power by affirming the broad interpretation of the Necessary and Proper Clause. Federal government could exercise implied powers to carry out its enumerated powers.

Implication of federal power necessary and proper to implement express aims and powers of the federation can be found in the Federalist Papers, Federalist No. 33 where Hamilton discusses the necessary and proper clause: "It may be affirmed with perfect confidence that the constitutional operation of the intended government would be precisely the same, if these clauses [the necessary and proper clause] were entirely obliterated, as if they were repeated in every article. They are only declaratory of a truth which would have resulted by necessary and unavoidable implication from the very act of constituting a federal government, and vesting it with certain specified powers." (Federalist No. 33). Article I, Section 8, Clause 18 of the United States Constitution.

Mnemonics: means ends rational review with strict scrutiny for suspect classes & fundamental rights. MERRSSSCFR. mere rational, strict suspect. fun right?

McCulloch, a cashier with a legal test,
Maryland's tax, he couldn't digest.
The Court stepped in, with a witty decree,
Federal supremacy, for all to see.

We just saw Marshall "tag team" the States with the elastic clause and the supremacy clause. Can you briefly restate those two basic constitutional rules?

The elastic clause, also known as the "necessary and proper" clause is a piece of explicit text written into the express terms of the constitution. It is the basis for the extension of express federal powers into implied powers. "The Congress shall have Power...To make all Laws which shall be necessary and proper for carrying into Execution the foregoing Powers, and all other Powers vested by this Constitution in the Government of the United States, or in any Department or Officer thereof." Article I, Section 8, Clause 18 of the United States Constitution. The supremacy clause holds that in a conflict between federal and state law the federal law must prevail provided of course the federal law is constitutional. The Constitution, federal laws, and treaties of the United States are the supreme law of the land. "This Constitution, and the Laws of the United States which shall be made in Pursuance thereof; and all Treaties made, or which shall be made, under the Authority of the United States, shall be the supreme Law of the Land; and the Judges in every State shall be bound thereby, any Thing in the Constitution or Laws of any State to the Contrary notwithstanding." Article VI, Clause 2 of the United States Constitution.

Elastic Clause: *Elasticity's key, powers expanded, you see!*

Supremacy Clause: *Supreme Law, no flaw, that's the Clause we saw!*

Are State and Federal powers respectively mutually exclusive or can there be concurrent federal and state power?

There are enumerated exclusive federal and state powers. In principle, as a general rule, Federal power is limited to international and inter-state relations, including relations with the various Indian Tribes (First Nations). State power in contrast is in principle plenary and extends to all fields. There may be specific exceptions. However, in theory States and Federal law should only clash in cases where the state seeks to enter into foreign or inter-state affairs or in cases where the federation chose to roam outside the fields of foreign and inter-state relations. Yet in practice the capacity of the federation to expand its powers by way of the elastic clause and the commerce clause creates many potential conflicts between federal and state law. Where the federal power is exercised lawfully and constitutionally these conflicts are determined in favor of the federation due to the supremacy clause. Thus there may be concurrent powers, which may or may not clash.

Name the express exclusive federal powers.

Exclusive federal powers are those powers that are specifically granted to the federal government and are not shared with the states. These powers are enumerated in the United States Constitution. Here are the most important examples of exclusive federal powers.

1. Interstate Commerce: Article I, Section 8, Clause 3 of the United States Constitution, also known as the Commerce Clause, grants Congress the authority "To regulate Commerce with foreign Nations, and among the several States, and with the Indian Tribes."

2. Coinage (Monetary Power): Congress has the power to coin money and regulate its value. The power "To coin Money, regulate the Value thereof, and of foreign Coin, and fix the Standard of Weights and Measures." Article I, Section 8, Clause 5 U.S. Const.

3. Immigration, Citizenship, Bankruptcy: "To establish an uniform Rule of Naturalization, and uniform Laws on the subject of Bankruptcies throughout the United States." Article I, Section 8, Clause 4

4. War Powers: Congress has right to declare legal wars. The President has the power to wage undeclared wars. "To declare War, grant Letters of Marque and Reprisal, and make Rules concerning Captures on Land and Water." Article I, Section 8, Clause 11 U.S. Const. This may however be seen as a concurrent power since the States do have the power to raise a militia and the people have the right to bear arms for militia service.

Are there any exclusively state powers? If so, name them.

"The powers not delegated to the United States by the Constitution, nor prohibited by it to the States, are reserved to the States respectively, or to the people." Tenth Amendment, U.S. Const. This is consistent with the idea that the U.S. federal government is a limited government of enumerated powers whereas the several states enjoy plenary power. State powers are presumed, whereas federal power must be proven. Consequently, the Tenth Amendment itself does not provide an exhaustive list of exclusive state powers, it establishes the principle of federalism and states' rights. States have the authority to regulate and govern in areas that are not explicitly under federal control. Thus in principle private law is state law whereas federal law is public law. There are many exceptions to this broad general rule.

"This government is acknowledged by all to be one of enumerated powers. The principle, that it can exercise only the powers granted to it, would seem too apparent to have required to be enforced by all those arguments, which its enlightened friends, while it was depending before the people, found it necessary to urge. That principle is now universally admitted." McCulloch v. Maryland, 17 U.S. (4 Wheat.) 316 (1819)

"The Constitution creates a Federal Government of enumerated powers. As James Madison wrote, '[t]he powers delegated by the proposed Constitution to the federal government are few and defined. Those which are to remain in the State governments are numerous and indefinite.'" United States v. Lopez, 514 U.S. 549 (1995).

What is the first or most important case to extend federal power by a "tag team" of the commerce clause and the elastic clause ("necessary and proper")?

Perhaps the first and certainly one of the most important cases that extended federal power through the combination of the Commerce Clause and the Necessary and Proper Clause is "Gibbons v. Ogden" (1824). Facts: In "Gibbons v. Ogden," the Supreme Court addressed a dispute over steamboat operations between Thomas Gibbons and Aaron Ogden. Ogden had been granted a monopoly by the state of New York to operate steamboats on certain waterways, while Gibbons held a federal license to operate steamboats along the same routes under a federal law regulating coastal trade.

Held: Commerce Clause of the Constitution granted Congress the power to regulate interstate commerce, including navigation on waterways shared by multiple states. Federal power to regulate commerce was enjoys supremacy over state laws that impeded or conflicted with it. "Gibbons v. Ogden" emphasized the broad interpretation of the Commerce Clause, stating that it encompassed not only the actual buying and selling of goods but also all the activities that facilitated and were necessary for commerce to occur. This expansive interpretation of the Commerce Clause, coupled with the Necessary and Proper Clause, empowered the federal government to regulate various aspects of interstate commerce and expand its authority in economic matters. Commerce is not merely buying and selling, it is also at least transporting goods, and even their production.

Memory aids: "Navigating Federal Waters, State Monopoly Shattered":

"Navigating Federal Waters" represents the interstate steamboat operations regulated by the federal government. "State Monopoly Shattered" signifies the Court's decision to invalidate the state-granted monopoly and assert federal authority over interstate commerce. The common law abhors monopoly. (See, e.g. Egerton's Case 4 HLC 1, 4 HL Cas. 1 – 1853; Packwood v. Briggs & Stratton Corp., 195 F. 2d 971 - Court of Appeals, 3rd Circuit 1952)

Monopolies and other restraints on trade are disfavored at common law (Standard Oil Co. of NJ v. United Sates, 221 US 1 - Supreme Court 1911), which is the unwritten constitution, that the U.S. written constitution codified (Marbury v. Madison, 5 US 137 - Supreme Court 1803). One may thus argue that disfavoring restraints on trade, one of the most important keys to Anglo-American wealth, is a constitutional principle. State hindrances to interstate and international commerce are thus very likely to fall whether because of intruding on exclusive federal power or because of their uneconomical character and burdening the fundamental rights to property and to freely enter into contracts.

Memory Techniques:

Gibbons and Ogden, in a steamboat race,
Clashed in court, seeking legal grace.
Commerce Clause prevailed, federal power did grow,
Interstate trade the states can't overthrow.

Gibbons and Ogden, in a legal bout,
The Court must decide what commerce is about.
Federal power won, state monopoly was tossed,
The Commerce Clause triumphed, leaving Ogden lost.

What is the establishment clause? What is the general test for determining whether a law violates the establishment clause of the First Amendment?

Answer: "Congress shall make no law respecting an establishment of religion, or prohibiting the free exercise thereof". U.S. Const., 1st Amendment.

The general test for evaluating whether a law violates the establishment clause is known as the Lemon Test. This test, derived from the Supreme Court case Lemon v. Kurtzman, 403 U.S. 602 (1971) provides a three-pronged analysis to assess the constitutionality of a law which may tend to establish an official state religion:

1. Excessive government entanglement with religion: The law must not result in excessive entanglement between government and religion. Funding religion, using religious institutions to perform government functions, those acts which tend to establish an official government religion and which violate the principle of separation of Church and State are unconstitutionally prohibited to prevent religious wars and oppression of religion, notably of religious minorities.

2. Secular purpose: Law must have a secular purpose, it must not have a religious objective.

3. Primary effect neither promotes nor inhibits religion: The primary effect of the law must neither advance nor inhibit religion. Religiously neutral laws can be constitutional.

If any of these prongs are violated, the law is deemed unconstitutional and invalid under the establishment clause as tending to establish an official state religion to the injury of other religions and to the body politic by fostering religious conflict as opposed to religious freedom and harmony.

Why Separation of Church and State: The United States is a secular democratic federal republic enjoying the separation of church and state. The separation of church and state is intended to prevent religious wars and the suppression of any religion. Constant religious wars in Europe drove many Americans to flee from Europe for these peaceful shores. The plain meaning of the establishment clause is clear: "Congress shall make no law respecting an establishment of religion, or prohibiting the free exercise thereof". U.S. Const., 1st Amendment. Church and State are separate in this revolutionary governance system, unlike other countries, at least historically. Since the American revolution many other countries, most notably France, have also taken up the wise policy of separation of Church and State, which is intended to prevent religious war while enabling religious freedom.

Cite: Lemon v. Kurtzman, 403 U.S. 602 (1971). Constitutionality of state statutes that provided financial aid to non-public, primarily religious schools. Issue: whether a government action violates the Establishment Clause of the First Amendment. Lemon, a Pennsylvania taxpayer, argued that financial aid to religious schools violated the First Amendment's Establishment Clause, which prohibits the government from establishing or favoring any religion. The statutes allowed the state to reimburse private schools, including religious schools, for certain secular educational services, such as teacher salaries, textbooks, and instructional materials. Held: the state statutes violated the Establishment Clause. According to the Lemon test, government actions are permissible under the Establishment Clause if they have a secular purpose, their primary effect neither advances nor inhibits religion, and they do not result in excessive entanglement between government and religion. Applying the Lemon test to the state statutes in question, the Court found that the primary effect of the financial aid was to advance religion, and it excessively entangled the government with religious institutions. The Court concluded that the statutes violated the Establishment Clause because they did not have a secular purpose and had the effect of advancing religion. The main function of governance is prevention and resolution of various social conflicts in the here-and-now. This is a very different function from religion, which often concerns, or at least addresses, the hereafter.

Mnemonics: Excessive E.ntanglement, S.ecular P.urpose, N.eutral=ESPN at 1AM. "Entangled Secular Purpose Neutral ESPN is a sports network I religiously watch." Use whatever memory technique works for you, though repetition just about always works – eventually. So keep at it.

Who bears the burden of proof that there is a "rational basis" linking the means chosen by government and some permissible end of governance, the government or the person claiming a government act is unconstitutional?

Answer: When a government action is alleged to be unconstitutional the usual standard of review is that there must be a rational relationship between the means chosen by the government and some end, which is a permissible goal of governance. That is rational basis review. The burden of proof in such cases rests on the plaintiff. Governmental action is ordinarily presumed to be lawful and constitutional. The plaintiff must prove the challenged law or government action is not rationally related to a legitimate government interest. They must show that there is no reasonable justification for the law and that it violates their constitutional rights thereby. This is a very high standard. If the law's means and end are permissible and the law in some way tends to achieve that end then it is rational and the court will not review the legislator's legal act which, again, is presumed to be lawful. Again: The plaintiff must present evidence and arguments to persuade the court that the law is unconstitutional under the rational basis standard. These ideas about judicial review of the legality of ordinary legislation against the U.S. constitution are expressed in the Federalist papers, Marbury v. Madison, and McCulloch v. Maryland.

Who bears the burden of proof when reviewing a law against the constitution and applying intermediate or strict scrutiny?

Answer: When applying intermediate scrutiny, the burden of proof that the law challenged is in fact constitutional is shifted to the state. The state is must prove the challenged law or government action serves an important government interest and is substantially related to achieving that interest.

Similarly, when strict scrutiny is applied, the burden of proof is also on the state. The state must prove that the challenged law or government action is necessary to achieve a compelling government interest, and that there are no less restrictive alternatives available.

In contrast, in rational basis review, the burden of proof lies with the plaintiff. The plaintiff is responsible for showing that the law is not rationally related to a legitimate government interest, meaning there is no reasonable justification for the law and that it violates their constitutional rights.

What are the three main categories of laws that are subject to rational basis review?

Answer: It is easiest to understand rational review as the general rule, and applying to all laws, with specific exceptions for laws that infringe on fundamental rights, including the right to equal protection of law. Thus, if a fundamental right is infringed on, the State must prove the law is not only a rational means to a permissible end, but that the means chosen is narrowly tailored, that it is the least restrictive means, the means which invades the fundamental right as little as possible to pursue a compelling state interest. Typically then 1st and 4th Amendment infringements will trigger "strict scrutiny", so also will laws which burden discrete and insular politically powerless minorities; thus laws burdening religion and religious groupings, or which burden racial groups; gender as a political non minority only enjoys intermediate scrutiny. However, ordinarily legislation is subject only to means-ends rational review. The laws so treated may be summed up as:

1. Laws affecting non-suspect classes: Rational basis review is used to evaluate laws that do not involve suspect classifications based on race, religion, or other protected characteristics. These laws are examined to determine whether they have a rational relationship to a legitimate government interest.

2. General laws of equal applicability: Rational basis review is applied to general laws that have equal applicability to all individuals or groups. These laws typically pertain to areas such as social welfare, economic interests, and public safety. The court assesses whether there is a rational connection between the law and a legitimate government objective.

3. Laws that do not implicate fundamental rights: Rational basis review is use for laws that do not involve the infringement of fundamental rights. These laws are evaluated to determine whether

they are rationally related to a legitimate government interest, even if they may have some impact on individual liberties.

Understanding these three categories helps in identifying the appropriate level of scrutiny applied to laws under rational basis review.

Citation: City of Cleburne v. Cleburne Living Center, Inc., 473 U.S. 432 (1985). Zoning ordinance required a special use permit for operation of a group home for individuals with intellectual disabilities. Permit was denied by the City of Cleburne, Texas for a nonprofit organization, Cleburne Living Center, that sought to establish a group home for individuals with intellectual disabilities. The city based its decision on a zoning ordinance that required such a permit for the operation of a group home for the intellectually disabled. Cleburne Living Center argued that the ordinance violated the Equal Protection Clause of the Fourteenth Amendment.

Held: zoning ordinance violated the Equal Protection Clause. Legislative classifications based on disability are subject to a heightened level of scrutiny. The ordinance discriminatory in that there was no rational basis for treating the intellectually disabled differently from other groups seeking housing in the same residential zone.

Laws discriminating against individuals with intellectual disabilities must be evaluated under heightened scrutiny, requiring a compelling government interest and narrowly tailored means to achieve that interest. The Court recognized that individuals with intellectual disabilities are entitled to the same fundamental rights and equal protection under the law as others. Individuals with disabilities are entitled to equal protection and challenged discriminatory practices that hinder their ability to live and participate fully in society.

To which categories does intermediate scrutiny apply?

Answer: Intermediate scrutiny is applied to the following categories:

1. Gender classifications: Intermediate scrutiny is used to evaluate laws that classify individuals based on their gender. These laws are subject to a heightened level of scrutiny to ensure they meet constitutional standards.

2. Illegitimate children: Laws that differentiate between legitimate and illegitimate children are also subject to intermediate scrutiny. The court examines whether such laws serve an important government interest and are substantially related to achieving that interest.

3. Aliens (unless the law is regulated for immigration purposes by the federal government): Intermediate scrutiny is applied to laws that impact aliens, meaning individuals who are not citizens or nationals of the country. If the law is specifically related to immigration and regulated by the federal government, rational basis review is generally applied instead.

4. Commercial Speech

Citation: Plyler v. Doe, 457 U.S. 202 (1982): Constitutionality of a Texas law that denied public education funding to undocumented immigrant children. Texas implemented a statute that withheld state funds from local school districts for the education of undocumented immigrant children. The law required school districts to deny enrollment to these children or charge them tuition at the full cost of education. A group of undocumented immigrant children, represented by Peter Schey and others, filed a lawsuit challenging the law on the grounds that it violated the Equal Protection Clause of the Fourteenth Amendment.

Held: Texas law violated the Equal Protection Clause. The Federal Constitution does not guarantee education as a fundamental right for all individuals, however once a state chooses to provide education to its residents, it cannot deny certain groups of children, such as undocumented immigrants, equal access to public education. Texas law imposed a significant burden on the affected children and created a subclass of people who would be denied educational opportunities solely based on their immigration status. The decision highlighted the importance of education in fostering individual development and contributing to the overall well-being of society. It concluded that denying education to undocumented immigrant children would perpetuate a disadvantaged underclass, which is contrary to the principles of equal protection. Undocumented immigrant children have the right to receive a public education on an equal basis with their peers.

The Equal Protection Clause applies to all individuals within a state's jurisdiction, regardless of their immigration status. Non-Citizens, at least on U.S. soil, but perhaps also overseas, enjoy fundamental constitutional rights, though do not enjoy all the political and civil rights of citizens, notably the right to vote.

What burden does the strict scrutiny standard impose?

Answer:

The strict scrutiny standard imposes a significant burden on the state. Under strict scrutiny, the state must demonstrate that the challenged law or government action is necessary to further a compelling government interest.

In order for a law to pass strict scrutiny, the state must satisfy two key requirements. First, the government interest involved must serve a compelling interest. Second, the law must be narrowly tailored, meaning it must be specifically designed to achieve that compelling interest and no less restrictive alternatives should be available.

The burden of proof lies with the state to provide strong justifications and evidence to meet the rigorous standards of strict scrutiny. This ensures that laws infringing upon fundamental rights or involving suspect classifications are subjected to a thorough examination to safeguard individual liberties.

Citation: Loving v. Virginia, 388 U.S. 1 (1967) Miscegenation is an insulting term for race mixing, which is also not a kind way to refer to mixed race people, which is at least a neutral description. Interracial is perhaps the least stigmatic term. Regardless, Loving v. Virginia, 388 U.S. 1 (1967), struck down laws prohibiting interracial marriage in the United States. The lovings, an interracial couple, were residents of Virginia. They were married in the District of Columbia, where interracial marriage was legal. When in Virginia, they were charged with violating the state's laws prohibiting "miscegenation" (that term is pejorative). The Lovings pled guilty and were sentenced to one year in prison, with the sentence suspended on the condition that they leave Virginia and not return together for 25 years.

The Lovings challenged their convictions, arguing that Virginia's anti-miscegenation laws violated the Equal Protection and Due Process Clauses of the Fourteenth Amendment. The Supreme Court unanimously agreed with the Lovings and held: Virginia laws unconstitutional. Marriage is a fundamental right; freedom to marry is a fundamental aspect of personal liberty. Laws prohibiting interracial marriage are based on racial classifications and therefore subject to strict scrutiny, the highest level of judicial review. Virginia's justifications for the anti-miscegenation laws, preserving racial purity or preventing social tensions, were not sufficiently compelling to justify the serious infringement on the Lovings' personal fundamental rights.

What is the presumption associated with strict scrutiny when it is applied to a law?

When strict scrutiny is implicated in the analysis of a law, there is a presumption that the law is unconstitutional. This means that the burden is initially placed on the government to provide a compelling justification for the law's constitutionality: the court scrutinizes the law rigorously to ensure that it serves a compelling government interest and is narrowly tailored to achieve that interest. The presumption of unconstitutionality is a high standard that the government must meet to justify the law's infringement on fundamental rights or involvement of suspect classifications. This presumption does not automatically render the law invalid. Instead, it sets a demanding threshold that the government must overcome to demonstrate the law's constitutionality.

Citation: Reed v. Reed, 404 U.S. 71 (1971). Sally Reed, mother of two children, and Cecil Reed, the children's father: their son died, both parents sought to be appointed as administrators of their son's estate. Under Idaho law, when multiple individuals sought appointment as administrators, males were given preference over females. Sally Reed's application for appointment was denied solely based on her gender. Sally Reed challenged the Idaho law, arguing that it violated the Equal Protection Clause by discriminating against her based on her gender. The Supreme Court, in a unanimous decision, held that the Idaho law violated the Equal Protection Clause.

Held: classifications based on gender were subject to an intermediate level of scrutiny, requiring that the classification be substantially related to an important governmental interest. Idaho law's gender-based preference lacked a rational basis and did not meet this standard. Equal Protection Clause prohibits arbitrary and invidious discrimination based on gender.

Reed v. Reed established a precedent that laws treating men and women differently must be based on an important governmental interest and must be substantially related to achieving that interest.

Which suspect classes are protected by strict scrutiny review?

Answer:

Strict scrutiny review protects the following suspect classes:

1. Races: Laws that classify individuals based on their race are subject to strict scrutiny. Such classifications are closely examined to ensure they serve a compelling government interest and are narrowly tailored to achieve that interest.

2. National Origin: Laws that differentiate individuals based on their national origin also receive strict scrutiny. The government must demonstrate a compelling interest and show that the law is narrowly tailored to further that interest.

3. Laws affecting fundamental rights: Though not a "suspect class" laws infringing on fundamental rights (individual inalienable rights) are subject to Strict scrutiny.
The court closely scrutinizes these laws to ensure they serve a compelling government interest and are narrowly tailored to protect those rights, that they are strictly necessary.

Relevant Case Citation: Loving v. Virginia, 388 U.S. 1 (1967), the summary thereof is in the prior question's answer.

Memorization Mnemonic: Fun Race NO? (Fundamental rights, Race, National Origin)
Stanley Kubrick RACING a "Loving" couple through a maze for ever and ever and ever...

What is "Commercial Speech"?

Answer: "Commercial speech" is speech that primarily proposes a commercial transaction or relates to an economic activity. Commercial speech typically involves advertisements, promotional materials, or other forms of communication aimed at promoting commercial goods, services, or activities.

An example of commercial speech would be a television advertisement for a particular brand of soda. The ad's purpose is to persuade viewers to purchase the soda, making it a form of commercial expression. The leading cases include:

1. Central Hudson Gas & Electric Corp. v. Public Service Commission of New York, 447 U.S. 557 (1980): In this case, the Supreme Court established a four-part test to determine the constitutionality of regulations on commercial speech. The Central Hudson test assesses whether the government's regulations directly advance a substantial government interest and are not more extensive than necessary.

2. Virginia State Board of Pharmacy v. Virginia Citizens Consumer Council, Inc., 425 U.S. 748 (1976): This case established that the First Amendment's protection extends to commercial speech and struck down a state law prohibiting pharmacists from advertising prescription drug prices.

3. Lorillard Tobacco Co. v. Reilly, 533 U.S. 525 (2001): The Supreme Court held that a Massachusetts regulation banning outdoor tobacco advertising within a specified distance of schools and playgrounds was unconstitutional because it was not narrowly tailored.

Mnemonics: PCT Econ Ex, % econ X, "propose commercial transaction economic exchange": your ex proposes, but really only wants a commercial exchange...

Are states permitted to pass laws that limit commercial speech?

Answer: Yes, states are allowed to pass laws that impose limitations on commercial speech, but certain conditions must be met for such restrictions to be constitutional. Commercial speech is afforded some protection under the First Amendment, although it is subject to a lower level of scrutiny compared to other forms of speech.

To pass constitutional muster, laws limiting commercial speech must meet specific criteria. They are permissible if they target speech that is fraudulent, misleading, or if the nature of the commerce involved is illegal. In these instances, the government has a substantial interest in regulating such speech to protect consumers, maintain fair competition, or prevent illegal activities.

Relevant Case Citation: Central Hudson Gas & Electric Corp. v. Public Service Commission, 447 U.S. 557 (1980)

Memorization Mnemonic: FLIM FLAM, FRAUDM ILL, FLM (Fraudulent, Misleading, Illegal Nature)

Exam Tip: When studying commercial speech and its limitations, remember the mnemonic FLM (Fraudulent, Misleading, Illegal Nature) to recall the permissible grounds for restricting commercial speech. Additionally, understanding the Central Hudson test established in Central Hudson Gas & Electric Corp. v. Public Service Commission is central to analyzing the constitutionality of laws limiting commercial speech. Is the exam question similar to the facts in Central Hudson? Does the exam question enable you to question, extend, or argue against the Central Hudson test? Or instead is the question "merely" wanting you to apply Central Hudson?

Is commercial speech subject to strict scrutiny, intermediate scrutiny, or rational review (means-ends) review?

Answer:

In U.S. constitutional law commercial speech is subject to intermediate scrutiny rather than strict scrutiny or rational review (means-ends) review.

The Supreme Court established the intermediate scrutiny standard of review in "Central Hudson test" for assessing regulations on commercial speech. Under the Central Hudson test, the government must meet a four-part analysis to determine the constitutionality of regulations on commercial speech:

1. Is the speech protected by the First Amendment? The speech must fall within the definition of commercial speech. Obscenity is not commercial speech, for example, obscenity is entirely unprotected.

2. Does the government have a **substantial** *interest* in regulating the speech?

3. Does the regulation directly advance the government's interest?

4. Is the regulation no more extensive than necessary to serve that interest? ("narrowly tailored" "least restrictive means")

If the government can demonstrate that the regulation satisfies these four criteria, it will be deemed constitutional under intermediate scrutiny. However, if any of these criteria are not met, the regulation may be deemed unconstitutional.

Although content neutral regulations of commercial speech are subject to intermediate scrutiny, certain types of commercial speech, such as false or misleading advertising, receive less or even no protection. Defamation, provocations such as incitement, threats, "fighting words", sedition, and child pornography are not considered "speech" are also unprotected by the first amendment.

Case: In MD II Entertainment, Inc. v. Dallas, 28 F.3d 492 n. 21 (5th Cir. 1994). Strip club restricted by zoning. Though the performances might be "speech" it is "commercial" (proposes a commercial transaction, an economic exchange) thus subject only to intermediate scrutiny.

Magic words: ("govern[s] content-neutral regulations of commercial speech")

What are the two primary factors considered when determining the constitutionality of restrictions on commercial speech?

Answer: When evaluating the constitutionality of restrictions on commercial speech, two main factors are taken into account:

1. Legal? Whether the commercial activity implicated is lawful: One factor considered is whether the commercial activity involved in the speech is lawful. If the nature of the commerce is illegal or inherently fraudulent, greater restrictions on the speech may be justified to protect the public interest.

2. Misleading? Whether the commercial speech is misleading: Another factor examined is whether the commercial speech is misleading. If the speech contains false or deceptive information that could potentially harm consumers or undermine fair competition, regulations aimed at curbing such misleading speech may be deemed constitutional.

Memorization Trick: Miss Leading Illegal Transaction. A pretty young woman lying her face off and trying to talk you into an illegal transaction. Ok, she's not young, I did say she is lying and thus UNPROTECTED.

Relevant Case Citation: Central Hudson Gas & Electric Corp. v. Public Service Commission, 447 U.S. 557 (1980). Restrictions on commercial speech. Central Hudson Gas & Electric Corp. challenged a regulation imposed by the Public Service Commission of New York that prohibited promotional advertising for electricity use intended to stimulate the demand for electricity.
Held: four-part test to determine the constitutionality of restrictions on commercial speech.

1. Is the speech protected by the First Amendment? The Court recognized that commercial speech, while receiving less protection than other forms of expression, is still entitled to constitutional protection.

2. Is the government interest in regulating the speech substantial? The Court required the government to demonstrate a substantial interest in regulating the particular expression at issue.

3. Does the regulation directly advance the government's interest? The Court required that the regulation must directly advance the government's asserted interest, meaning there must be a clear and reasonable connection between the regulation and the government's objective.

4. Is the regulation no more extensive than necessary to serve the government's interest? The Court required that the regulation must be narrowly tailored, meaning it should not burden more speech than necessary to achieve the government's objective.

Regulation violated the First Amendment. Although government had a substantial interest in conserving energy, the regulation was not sufficiently tailored to achieve that interest. The prohibition on promotional advertising was deemed too broad and restricted more speech than necessary.

What requirements must be met by a law that limits commercial speech if the speech is neither misleading nor illegal?

Answer: If commercial speech is neither misleading nor illegal, a law that limits such speech must pass intermediate scrutiny. The law must be reviewed under the intermediate scrutiny standard, which requires that the restriction is substantially related to an important government interest. There must be a legitimate and significant reason for the government to restrict the commercial speech.

1. The law must be narrowly tailored: The restriction imposed by the law must be narrowly tailored, meaning it should be specifically designed to achieve the government's interest. It should not be overly broad or unnecessary in limiting speech rights. Additionally, the law should leave open alternative means of communication, ensuring that individuals have other avenues to express their commercial messages.

2. There must be a logical nexus: There must be a logical nexus or connection between the narrowly tailored law and the purpose of the legislation. This requirement ensures that the restriction directly advances the government interest in a reasonable and coherent manner.

Relevant Case Citation: Central Hudson Gas & Electric Corp. v. Public Service Commission, 447 U.S. 557 (1980) (see prior question's answer for the summary).

Memorization Mnemonic: IS narrow nexus (Intermediate scrutiny, Narrowly tailored, Logical nexus), ISNN, ISNTLN; Intermediate Commercial, Commercial Intermediary

What is the purpose of the equal protection clause? How does it function?

Answer: The equal protection clause ensures like things are not treated differently by law. This is a procedural equality, not substantive. You are free to be rich or poor and are not compelled to economic equality. However, the law regards all persons of equal dignity, having equal procedural rights. The equal protection clause, found in the Fourteenth Amendment of the United States Constitution, mandates that state laws must treat similarly situated individuals or classes of people equally. The clause serves to ensure fairness and prohibits laws that unjustifiably treat people unequally. Equal protection most notably protects different races but also protects different religions, ethnicities ("No Irish Need Apply"), or any other arbitrary discrimination. Laws regulating "left handed pipefitters from Cleveland" likely would violate equal protection, since there is no rational basis for regulating left handers any more than there is for regulating Irish, Chinese, or mixed-race persons. When a law treats individuals or classes unequally, it is generally considered unconstitutional and invalid under the equal protection clause. This means that the government must have some compelling state interest which justifies differentiating between individuals or classes, and the law must be narrowly tailored to achieve that purpose.

Relevant Case Citation: Brown v. Board of Education, 347 U.S. 483 (1954). Unconstitutionality of racial segregation in public schools. African American families filed lawsuits challenging the constitutionality of segregated public schools. Supreme Court consolidated the cases into one proceeding. Issue: whether the "separate but equal" doctrine established in Plessy v. Ferguson (1896) should be overturned. The doctrine allowed for racially segregated facilities as long as they were deemed equal in quality.

Held: racial segregation in public schools violated the Equal Protection Clause of the Fourteenth Amendment. "Separate but equal" had no place in public education, segregation inherently created feelings of inferiority among African American children. Court concluded that segregated educational facilities were inherently unequal and deprived African American children of equal educational opportunities.

Memorization Mnemonic: Brown skinned kids treated separately thus unequally, unfair, no fun for anyone. Legally obligated segregation violates equal protection of the nation.

What is the standard of review applied when equal protection is at issue?

Answer: The standard of review applied when equal protection is at issue depends on the classification or class being considered. Different classes receive different levels of scrutiny:

1. Strict scrutiny: When a law or government action involves classifications based on suspect classes such as race or national origin, the strict scrutiny standard is applied. Under strict scrutiny, the government must demonstrate that the law serves a compelling government interest and is narrowly tailored to achieve that interest.

2. Rational basis: For classifications based on non-suspect classes, such as age or income level, the rational basis standard is used. Under rational basis review, the government must show that the law is rationally related to a legitimate government interest.

3. Intermediate Scrutiny: Gender, Legitimacy/Orphans/Adoptions, Commercial speech

Relevant Case Citation: Korematsu v. United States, 323 U.S. 214 (1944). Japanese internment in concentration camps during World War II. United States government issued an executive order that authorized forced relocation and internment of Japanese Americans from the West Coast into internment camps. Korematsu, an American citizen of Japanese descent, violated the order and was arrested and convicted therefor. He challenged the constitutionality of his conviction, arguing that the internment of Japanese Americans violated the Equal Protection Clause of the Fourteenth Amendment. The U.S. Supreme Court upheld Korematsu's conviction and found that the forced relocation and internment of Japanese Americans were justified as a military necessity during wartime. The Court applied strict scrutiny, to analyze the constitutionality of the government's actions. However, it ultimately ruled that the need to protect against espionage and sabotage outweighed the individual rights of Japanese Americans. Aftermath: In 1988, the United States Congress passed the Civil Liberties Act, officially apologizing for the internment and providing reparations to surviving Japanese Americans who were interned. In 2018, the Supreme Court officially overruled Korematsu v. United States in Trump v. Hawaii, recognizing the decision as "gravely wrong" and repudiating the reasoning behind it. Do it for George Takei.

Memorization Mnemonic: RRSS (Rational Review, Strict scrutiny) RR railroad SS the bad guys in WW2. "HeRR HanSS ... are we the baddies?" "Ja." George Takei shaking, shaking his head, George Takei pointing, pointing his finger. He is STRICTLY SCRUTINIZING You.

What is the standard of review used when determining the constitutionality of a law under the equal protection clause?

Answer: The standard of review employed to assess the constitutionality of a law under the equal protection clause depends on the classification or class involved. Different standards of review are applied:

1. Rational basis: For classifications based on non-suspect classes, such as age or income level, the rational basis standard is applied. In this context, the government is required to show that the law is rationally related to a legitimate government interest.

2. Intermediate scrutiny: applies to "semi-suspect" classifications like adoptions, gender, and also to commercial speech.

3. Strict scrutiny: When a law or government action involves classifications based on suspect classes such as race or national origin, the strict scrutiny standard is utilized. Under strict scrutiny, the government must demonstrate that the law serves a compelling government interest and is narrowly tailored to achieve that interest.

It is important to understand that these standards of review determine the level of scrutiny and the burden of justification placed on the government when analyzing equal protection claims.

Relevant Case Citation: Korematsu v. United States, 323 U.S. 214 (1944)

Memorization Mnemonic: SSRA (Strict Scrutiny, Rational Review)

What are the requirements that must be met by laws limiting speech in a private forum and a limited public forum?

Answer: Laws that restrict speech in a private forum and a limited public forum must satisfy the following requirements:

1. The law must be "reasonably" related to a legitimate government purpose: The restriction imposed by the law must have a rational basis or a reasonable connection to a legitimate government interest. This means that the government must demonstrate a valid reason for limiting speech in these forums, and the restriction must be reasonably related to achieving that purpose.

2. The limitation must be viewpoint neutral: The restriction on speech must be applied in a viewpoint-neutral manner. This means that the government cannot favor or disfavor specific viewpoints or perspectives. The law must treat all viewpoints equally and should not discriminate based on the content or message conveyed.

These requirements ensure that laws limiting speech in private and limited public forums uphold the principles of fairness and do not unduly infringe on individuals' freedom of expression.

Relevant Case Citation: Perry Education Association v. Perry Local Educators' Association, 460 U.S. 37 (1983)

"In places which by long tradition or by government fiat have been devoted to assembly and debate, the rights of the State to limit expressive activity are sharply circumscribed. At one end of the spectrum are streets and parks which 'have immemorially been held in trust for the use of the public and, time out of mind, have been used for purposes of assembly, communicating thoughts between citizens, and discussing public questions.' Hague v. CIO, 307 U. S. 496, 515 (1939). In these quintessential public forums, the government may not prohibit all communicative activity. For the State to enforce a content-based exclusion it must show that its regulation is necessary to serve a compelling state interest and that it is narrowly drawn to achieve that end. Carey v. Brown, 447 U. S. 455, 461 (1980). The State may also enforce regulations of the time, place, and manner of expression which are content-neutral, are narrowly tailored to serve a significant government interest, and leave open ample alternative channels of communication. United States Postal Service v. Council of Greenburgh Civic Assns., 453 U. S. 114, 132 (1981); Consolidated Edison Co. v. Public Service Comm'n, 447 U. S. 530, 535-536 (1980); Grayned v. City of Rockford, supra, at 115; Cantwell v. Connecticut, 310 U. S. 296 (1940); Schneider v. State, 308 U. S. 147 (1939).

A second category consists of public property which the State has opened for use by the public as a place for expressive activity. The Constitution forbids a State to enforce certain exclusions from a forum generally open to the public even if it was not required to create the forum in the first place. Widmar v. Vincent, 454 U. S. 263 (1981) (university meeting facilities); City of Madison Joint School District v. Wisconsin Employment Relations Comm'n, 429 U. S. 167 (1976) (school board meeting); Southeastern Promotions, Ltd. v. Conrad, 420 U. S. 546 (1975) (municipal the*46ater).7 Although a State is not required to indefinitely retain the open character of the facility, as long as it does so it is bound by the same standards as apply in a traditional public forum. Reasonable time, place, and manner regulations are permissible, and a content-based prohibition must be narrowly drawn to effectuate a compelling state interest. Widmar v. Vincent, supra, at 269-270.

Public property which is not by tradition or designation a forum for public communication is governed by different standards. We have recognized that the 'First Amendment does not guarantee access to property simply because it is owned or controlled by the government.' United States Postal Service v. Council of Greenburgh

Civic Assns., supra, at 129. In addition to time, place, and manner regulations, the State may reserve the forum for its intended purposes, communicative or otherwise, as long as the regulation on speech is reasonable and not an effort to suppress expression merely because public officials oppose the speaker's view. 453 U. S., at 131, n. 7. ... '[t]he State, no less than a private owner of property, has power to preserve the property under its control for the use to which it is lawfully dedicated.' ' ' Id., at 129-130, quoting Greer v. Spock, 424 U. S. 828, 836 (1976), in turn quoting Adderley v. Florida, 385 U. S. 39, 47 (1966)."

What are the requirements that must be satisfied by laws that restrict speech in a public forum?

Answer: Laws that limit speech in a public forum must meet the Time, Place, Manner Test:

1. The law must be content neutral: The restriction on speech should not be based on the content or viewpoint expressed. The government cannot favor or disfavor particular ideas or messages. Instead, the law must apply equally to all types of speech.

2. The law must be narrowly tailored to serve an important government interest: The restriction imposed by the law must be carefully crafted and precisely tailored to achieve a significant government interest. The government must demonstrate that there is a compelling need to regulate speech in a particular manner.

3. The law must leave open alternative methods for communicating the message: Individuals affected by the restriction must still have reasonable alternative avenues available to express their message or convey their ideas. The law should not completely prohibit or foreclose all opportunities for communication.

Relevant Case Citation: Ward v. Rock Against Racism, 491 U.S. 781 (1989)

Ward v. Rock Against Racism, 491 U.S. 781 (1989): constitutionality of time, place, and manner restrictions on free speech. Facts: a public concert. Dispute between Rock Against Racism (RAR), an organization that organized live music events promoting racial tolerance, and Thomas Ward, the commissioner of the New York City Department of Parks and Recreation. RAR sought to hold a concert in Central Park. NYCDPR imposed certain restrictions on the event, including use of a city-operated sound system and sound technician to be assigned by the city.

Held: time, place, and manner restrictions in this case were constitutional. Although public parks are traditional public fora for free expression, the government has the authority to impose reasonable restrictions to ensure that speech does not interfere with others' legitimate interests, such as public safety and the enjoyment of the park by others.

The Court established a four-part test to evaluate the constitutionality of time, place, and manner restrictions. The restrictions must be content-neutral, narrowly tailored to serve a significant government interest, leave open ample alternative channels for communication, and provide reasonable standards for officials applying the restrictions.

Applying the test to the case, the Court found that the restrictions imposed by the department met these criteria. The use of a city-operated sound system was necessary to control the volume and quality of sound to prevent noise disturbances in the park and surrounding areas. The requirement for a city-assigned sound technician ensured the proper functioning of the equipment. The restrictions did not target the content of the speech but were aimed at preserving public safety and the peaceful enjoyment of the park by other visitors.

Memorization Mnemonic: CNNTMA (Content neutral, Narrowly tailored, Method alternatives) Visualization: Watching CNN with mom in a narrowly tailored tuxedo in a public forum.

What is the State action requirement in relation to the protection of freedom of speech?

Answer: In principle the U.S. constitution is a public law instrument and thus only applies to public law entities like the Federation, the several States. There are many exceptions to this general rule. However, application of a constitutional right between private parties inter se, if allowed at all under the U.S. constitution would be very exceptional. Non-enforceability of racially restrictive property covenants are the only famous example of a U.S. constitutional provision affecting private rights, and even there the private law contract is not illegal, it is however unenforceable by the public power. This is consistent with the "void against public policy" exception to contractual enforcement.

The State action requirement, as it pertains to the safeguarding of freedom of speech under the First and Fourteenth Amendments, stipulates that constitutional protections are applicable only when there is a state action that restricts speech. It means that private entities, such as private clubs, have the constitutional authority to limit free speech without violating the First and Fourteenth Amendments. Private persons, including groups of persons whether as unincorporated associations or corporations are presumed to have the power to freely organize themselves and their interactions with other persons free from government intrusion into their private affairs. This is a core feature of the limited democratic government model which characterizes American democracy. Not every country does this by any means, and in fact such totalitarian states (for they exercise total power over all aspects of life) are often in conflict, sometimes armed, with the United States of America.

Relevant Case Citation: Marsh v. Alabama, 326 U.S. 501 (1946)

Marsh v. Alabama, 326 U.S. 501 (1946): extent of constitutional protections in privately owned company towns.

Marsh, a Jehovah's Witness, was distributing religious literature in Chickasaw, Alabama. Town was owned by Gulf Shipbuilding Corporation, operated as a company town: the corporation owned and controlled most of the property and businesses.

Marsh refused to stop distributing literature, was arrested for trespassing. Marsh challenged her conviction, arguing that her First Amendment rights to free speech and religious freedom had been violated.

Held: Chickasaw, despite being privately owned, was essentially a public forum, and therefore the First Amendment protections applied. The Court town functioned as the equivalent of a municipality, providing essential public services, and serving as the center of commerce and public life for the residents. As a result, the private ownership of the town did not justify the infringement on Marsh's constitutional rights. Rights guaranteed by the First Amendment must be protected in areas where individuals engage in the exercise of their liberties, even if those areas are owned by private entities. Certain "private" functions and spaces can become so integral to the community that they effectively become public fora, to which constitutional protection attaches.

What is the jurisdiction of the Supreme Court of the United States? What types of cases may it hear?

Answer: The Supreme Court of the United States has jurisdiction over the following types of cases:

1. Actions involving high-ranking government officials: The Supreme Court can hear cases involving high-ranking government officials, such as ambassadors. These cases often involve matters of significant national importance. Citation: U.S. Const. art. III, § 2, cl. 2 "In all Cases affecting Ambassadors, other public Ministers and Consuls, and those in which a State shall be Party, the supreme Court shall have original Jurisdiction."

2. Disputes between the federal government and a state: The Supreme Court has the authority to hear disputes that arise between the federal government and a state. These cases involve conflicts regarding the interpretation or application of federal law and the powers of the federal government. Citation: U.S. Const. art. III, § 2, cl. 2 "In all Cases [...] in which the United States shall be Party, the supreme Court shall have appellate Jurisdiction."

3. Disputes between two or more states: The Supreme Court can adjudicate disputes between two or more states. These cases typically involve conflicts related to boundaries, water rights, or other interstate issues. Citation: U.S. Const. art. III, § 2, cl. 2 "In all Cases [...] between two or more States [...] the supreme Court shall have original Jurisdiction."

4. Disputes involving an action by a state against citizens of another state or aliens of another state: The Supreme Court has jurisdiction over cases where a state brings a legal action against citizens of another state or aliens from another state. These cases often raise questions about the rights and privileges of individuals under the

Constitution. Citation: U.S. Const. art. III, § 2, cl. 1 Quote: "The judicial Power shall extend to all Cases, in Law and Equity, arising under this Constitution, the Laws of the United States, and Treaties made, or which shall be made, under their Authority;—to all Cases affecting Ambassadors, other public Ministers and Consuls;—to all Cases of admiralty and maritime Jurisdiction;—to Controversies to which the United States shall be a Party;—to Controversies between two or more States;—between a State and Citizens of another State, —between Citizens of different States,—between Citizens of the same State claiming Lands under Grants of different States, and between a State, or the Citizens thereof, and foreign States, Citizens or Subjects."

Relevant Case Citation: McCulloch v. Maryland, 17 U.S. 316 (1819). Scope and limits of federal power. Dispute between the state of Maryland and the Second Bank of the United States, a federally chartered bank. Maryland attempted to impose a tax on the bank, claiming the power to tax entities operating within its borders. The bank's cashier, James McCulloch, refused to pay the tax, leading to a legal challenge.

Held: 1. Maryland could not tax the federal bank.

2. The Necessary and Proper Clause: Congress possesses implied powers to carry out its enumerated powers under Article I, Section 8 of the Constitution. This provision, known as the Necessary and Proper Clause, grants Congress the authority to enact laws that are necessary and proper to fulfill its constitutional functions.

3. Supremacy of Federal Law: supremacy of federal law over state law. Marshall declared that "the power to tax involves the power to destroy" and rejected the idea that states could impede or undermine valid exercises of federal authority.

4. Federal Instrumentalities: Second Bank of the United States was a legitimate federal instrumentality created to carry out the

government's fiscal operations. Thus, Maryland's attempt to tax it would interfere with these essential federal functions. ("The power to tax is the power to destroy.")

Affirmed doctrine of implied powers, recognizing Congress possesses authority beyond its explicitly enumerated powers. Supremacy of federal law. Limited the ability of states to obstruct or interfere with legitimate federal institutions.

Memory key: The Supreme Court is the court which governs public law first and foremost. This means disputes between States, between the federation and a state, or even disputes between one of the several states and a private law person such as an individual human being or a corporate body and unincorporated associations.

Is Congress authorized to appoint officials for the purpose of enforcing acts of Congress?

Answer: No, Congress does not have the authority to appoint officials specifically for enforcing acts of Congress. The power to enforce laws is vested in the executive branch, the courts, or administrative officials. Congress's role primarily involves the creation and enactment of legislation, while the responsibility for enforcement rests with other branches or administrative bodies.

Relevant Case Citation: Humphrey's Executor v. United States, 295 U.S. 602 (1935). Limits of presidential authority in removing certain government officials. Mr. Humphrey, had been appointed as a member of the Federal Trade Commission (FTC) by President Franklin D. Roosevelt, but died. After Humphrey's death, his executor, Smith, sought to continue a lawsuit initiated by the late Mr. Humphrey against the United States. However, President Roosevelt sought to remove Humphrey's Executor from office.

Held: President did not possess the authority to remove a commissioner from an independent regulatory agency (here, the Federal Trade Commission) without cause because,

1. Independence of Regulatory Agencies: Certain regulatory agencies, including the FTC, were created by Congress to be independent and nonpartisan in their decision-making. These agencies were meant to carry out specific functions and were insulated from direct presidential control.

2. Limited Removal Power of the President: The Court distinguished between executive officials who serve at the pleasure of the President and officials with fixed terms or specific removal protections. It concluded that officials with certain protections in their tenure could not be removed by the President without cause.

3. Separation of Powers: Congress had the authority to structure independent agencies and limit the President's removal powers.

Humphrey's Executor v. United States recognized the need for independence and expertise in specialized regulatory bodies and protected them from potential political interference. Affirmed the separation of powers and the importance of checks and balances within the federal government.

What is meant by the term "inferior officer"?

Answer: "Inferior officer" are officers who serve under a federal administration.

Relevant Case Citation: Edmond v. United States, 520 U.S. 651 (1997) The Appointments Clause of Article II of the Constitution reads as follows:

*659"[The President] shall nominate, and by and with the Advice and Consent of the Senate, shall appoint Ambassadors, other public Ministers and Consuls, Judges of the supreme Court, and all other Officers of the United States, whose Appointments are not herein otherwise provided for, and which shall be established by Law: but the Congress may by Law vest the Appointment of such inferior Officers, as they think proper, in the President alone, in the Courts of Law, or in the Heads of Departments." U. S. Const., Art. II, §2, cl. 2.

"Our cases have not set forth an exclusive criterion for distinguishing between principal and inferior officers for Appointments Clause purposes. Among the offices that we have found to be inferior are that of a district court clerk, *Ex parte Hennen,* 13 Pet. 225, 258 (1839), an election supervisor, *Ex parte Siebold,* 100 U. S. 371, 397-398 (1880), a vice consul charged temporarily with the duties of the consul, *United States* v. *Eaton,* 169 U. S. 331, 343 (1898), and a "United States commissioner" in district court proceedings, *Go-Bart Importing Co.* v. *United States,* 282 U. S. 344, 352-354 (1931). Most recently, in *Morrison* v. *Olson,* 487 U. S. 654 (1988), we held that the independent counsel created by provisions of the Ethics in Government Act of 1978, 28 U. S. C. §§ 591-599, was an inferior officer. In reaching that conclusion, we relied on several factors: that the independent counsel was subject to removal by a higher officer (the Attorney General), that she performed only limited duties, that her jurisdiction was narrow, and that her tenure was limited. 487 U. S., at 671-672." Edmond v. United States, 520 U.S. 651 (1997)

"Generally speaking, the term "inferior officer" connotes a relationship with some higher ranking officer or officers below the President: Whether one is an "inferior" officer depends on whether he has a superior. It is not enough that other officers may be identified who formally maintain' a *663higher rank, or possess responsibilities of a greater magnitude. If that were the intention, the Constitution might have used the phrase "lesser officer." Rather, in the context of a Clause designed to preserve political accountability relative to important Government assignments, we think it evident that "inferior officers" are officers whose work is directed and supervised at some level by others who were appointed by Presidential nomination with the advice and consent of the Senate." Edmond v. United States, 520 U.S. 651 662-663 (1997).

Who has the constitutional authority to appoint inferior officers of the United States?

The President appoints superior officers. Inferior officers may be designated by congress to be appointed variously. The relevant constitutional provision follows:

"[The President] shall nominate, and by and with the Advice and Consent of the Senate, shall appoint Ambassadors, other public Ministers and Consuls, Judges of the supreme Court, and all other Officers of the United States, whose Appointments are not herein otherwise provided for, and which shall be established by Law: but the Congress may by Law vest the Appointment of such inferior Officers, as they think proper, in the President alone, in the Courts of Law, or in the Heads of Departments." U. S. Const., Art. II, §2, cl. 2.

What is procedural due process?

Answer: Procedural due process is the constitutional requirement that government actions that deprive a person of life, liberty, or property must adhere to fair procedures. It ensures that individuals are provided with **notice and an opportunity to be heard** before they are deprived of their rights or interests. Procedural due process rights include notice and an opportunity **to have a hearing, the right to call witnesses, cross-examine adverse witnesses, and be represented by counsel** if desired.

Relevant case citation: Goldberg v. Kelly, 397 U.S. 254 (1970): In this case, the Supreme Court held that individuals receiving public assistance benefits have a right to a pre-termination hearing before their benefits can be terminated. The Court emphasized the importance of procedural due process protections in safeguarding individuals' interests.

What factors are taken into account during a procedural due process analysis?

Answer: A procedural due process inquiry considers the following factors:

1. The significance of the individual rights that are being affected: The level of importance attached to the specific rights at stake.

2. The procedural safeguards for protecting those rights: an assessment of the procedural protections to ensure fairness and prevent arbitrary deprivation of rights.

3. The government's interest, whether at the state or federal level, in maintaining efficiency in the adjudicative process: The state or federal government's interest in the efficient administration of justice is considered while weighing the competing factors.

Relevant Case Citation: Mathews v. Eldridge, 424 U.S. 319 (1976). Procedural due process requires a balancing the individual's interests, the government's interests in limiting procedural burdens, the risk of mistakenly harming individual interests under existing procedures, and the potential benefit of additional procedures in reducing errors.

Test Tip: Understanding these factors and their balancing test is vital for analyzing procedural due process issues on your law exam. When discussing procedural due process, provide a thorough analysis by considering each of these factors and their interplay in the given scenario. Work creatively to link the facts in the test question to reasons for finding the given factor is or is not so important and then explain your justifications based on the facts for finding the given right is or is not infringed.

What are the two primary powers granted to the federal government under the commerce clause?

Answer: The federal government, under the commerce clause, possesses two main powers:

1. Plenary Power, i.e. full power, empowered to do all things necessary and proper, to regulate interstate commerce: The federal government has broad authority to regulate commercial activities that occur between states. This power allows for the regulation of various aspects of interstate commerce, including trade, transportation, and economic transactions.

2. Exclusive Authority to regulate foreign commerce: The federal government has the sole power to regulate commercial activities involving foreign nations. This includes the regulation of imports, exports, tariffs, and other aspects of international trade.

Relevant Case Citation: Gibbons v. Ogden, 22 U.S. 1 (1824)

Memorization Key: PPEXA Plenary Power, Exclusive Authority. Image: Peppa Pig being all selfish and exclusive about her commerce claws. Peppa Pig sells chicken claws oink snort

Load cotton on a paddlewheel steamer, send it up the river and its interstate commerce subject to complete federal regulation.

Problematique: A problematique is a question we ask ourselves to guide our learning. Here's the problematiques for the commerce power. What is commerce? What is interstate commerce? What is foreign commerce? When does in-state activity "affect" interstate commerce sufficiently to be subject to federal regulation under the commerce clause? Try to ask yourself the kinds of questions your examiner will ask you. Pretend you're the teacher, can you write model questions, and then model answers? Try to develop problematiques whenever you find an area of law you don't understand.

Exam Tip: To remember the powers granted to the federal government under the commerce clause, use the mnemonic PAIR (Plenary power, Absolute power, Interstate commerce, Regulate foreign commerce). Understand the extent (plenary) and limits (fundamental individual inalienable rights) of the federal government's authority in regulating commerce. Familiarize yourself with cases like Gibbons v. Ogden to gain insight into the relevant legal principles. Additionally, when discussing the commerce clause, provide a comprehensive analysis that encompasses both the power to regulate interstate commerce and the exclusive authority to regulate foreign commerce.

What is the extent of the president's foreign affairs power under Article II?

Answer: Under Article II of the Constitution, the president possesses exclusive authority to represent the United States in foreign affairs. This power is vested solely in the president, granting them the responsibility and discretion to act as the primary representative of the nation on the international stage. The President can undertake acts of war, enter into executive agreements, and sign treaties which he may then have ratified by congress to give such international law acts binding domestic legal effect.

Relevant Case Citation: United States v. Curtiss-Wright Export Corp., 299 U.S. 304 (1936)

Memory Key: The US President is a War Chief. He has the exclusive war power and foreign policy representation power so as to lead an effective united foreign policy. His domestic powers are frankly limited, but his foreign powers are untrammeled.

Exam Tip: When discussing the president's foreign affairs power, provide a thorough analysis of the exclusive authority granted to the president and their role as the representative of the United States in international relations.

What methods can the federal government employ to require a state to enact a particular legislative action?

Answer: The federal government does not possess the authority to compel a state to undertake any specific legislative action! This is because the Constitution grants the states the power to independently legislate within their respective jurisdictions. States, Tribes, and Federation are all Sovereigns. The federal government's role is limited to its enumerated powers and cannot directly dictate legislative actions to states. The several states are sovereigns, as is the federation and the various Indian tribes (first nations). The principle of sovereign equality means each sovereign cannot invade the others' sovereign rights. The federal government can however raise revenues and then distribute them to the several states contingent on the state's compliance with conditions.

Exam Tip: It is important to understand the limitations on the federal government's power to compel states in legislative matters. Remember that the Constitution grants states the authority to enact their own legislation within their respective jurisdictions. Being aware of this limitation will help you analyze questions related to federal-state relations and the scope of the federal government's power on your law exam.

Is it permissible for a private citizen to file a lawsuit against a state?

Answer: No, under the doctrine of sovereign immunity, a private citizen generally cannot sue a state in federal court without the state's consent. Sovereign immunity is a legal principle that protects states from being sued without their consent, based on the idea that states possess inherent sovereignty and should not be subjected to legal actions without their agreement.

What role does the Eleventh Amendment play in private citizens suing a state?

Answer: The Eleventh Amendment of th United States Constitution serves as a constitutional limitation on the ability of private citizens to sue a state. The amendment provides states with immunity from certain types of lawsuits filed by individuals in federal courts. It generally prohibits federal lawsuits against states by citizens of other states or foreign countries, unless the state specifically consents to being sued or Congress validly abrogates the state's immunity.

Relevant Case Citation: Seminole Tribe of Florida v. Florida, 517 U.S. 44 (1996). Issue: sovereign immunity and power of states to be sued by Indian tribes in federal court. The Seminole Tribe of Florida filed a lawsuit against the state of Florida, seeking to compel the state to negotiate in good faith for a compact to allow casino gambling on tribal lands. The Tribe relied on the Indian Gaming Regulatory Act (IGRA) as the basis for its claim.

Held: Eleventh Amendment to the United States Constitution barred the Seminole Tribe's lawsuit against the state of Florida. The Court concluded that Congress did not have the authority under the Commerce Clause to abrogate state sovereign immunity and subject states to lawsuits by Indian tribes in federal court. Seminole Tribe of Florida v. Florida reaffirmed the principle of state sovereign immunity, which protects states from being sued in federal court without their consent. The Court's ruling limited the power of Congress to abrogate state immunity under federal laws enacted pursuant to the Commerce Clause.

Name some of the most important recent Indian law Supreme Court cases.

1. City of Sherrill v. Oneida Indian Nation of New York, 544 U.S. 197 (2005):

Tribal land claims and the doctrine of laches. The Court held that the Oneida Indian Nation's claim to reacquire ancestral lands was barred by the doctrine of laches, which prevents a party from asserting a claim after an unreasonable delay. This was a bad decision.

A. Indian Gaming Regulatory Act (IGRA) Amendments: Since its enactment in 1988, the IGRA has undergone several amendments that have had a significant impact on tribal-state relations. These amendments clarified the regulatory framework for tribal gaming operations, established requirements for tribal-state compacts, and provided guidelines for revenue sharing and Class III gaming activities. Note: IGRA is Russian for game... draw your own conclusions.

3. Carcieri v. Salazar, 555 U.S. 379 (2009): Indian Reorganization Act of 1934 did not authorize the Secretary of the Interior to take land into trust for tribes recognized after 1934, limiting the ability of some tribes to acquire additional lands for economic or cultural purposes.

B. Violence Against Women Act (VAWA) Tribal Jurisdiction Provisions: In 2013, the reauthorization of the VAWA included provisions that recognized the inherent tribal authority to exercise criminal jurisdiction over non-Indians who commit domestic violence, dating violence, or violate protection orders on tribal lands. This legislation aimed to address jurisdictional gaps and improve the safety of Native American women.

4. McGirt v. Oklahoma, 591 U.S. ____ (2020): This Supreme Court case reaffirmed the boundaries of tribal reservations and recognized

the reservation of the Muscogee (Creek) Nation. The Court held that the reservation, as established by historical treaties, had not been disestablished by Congress, resulting in significant implications for criminal jurisdiction and coordination between tribal and state authorities.

Hopefully the court will revisit the Oneida claims; maybe also Seminole Tribe v. Florida. We The People aren't asking for anything other than the treaties and constitution be actually respected.

Under what circumstances can a citizen sue a state government?

Answer: The general rule is an individual cannot sue a State. Exceptionally, a citizen may sue a state government when seeking to enjoin a state official from enforcing a law that is deemed unconstitutional. This exception allows individuals to challenge the constitutionality of a state law and seek relief by preventing state officials from enforcing it.

Relevant Case Citation: Ex parte Young, 209 U.S. 123 (1908). Established an important exception to the Eleventh Amendment's general prohibition on suing a state in federal court. Held: A citizen can sue a state government official in their official capacity to seek an injunction, or a court order, preventing them from enforcing an allegedly unconstitutional state law. This exception allows individuals to challenge the constitutionality of state laws without directly suing the state itself, which would typically be barred by the Eleventh Amendment. The rationale behind the Ex parte Young doctrine is that when state officials act in violation of the federal Constitution, they are not truly acting on behalf of the state. Therefore, individuals can bring lawsuits against them to protect their federal rights.

Is the power to regulate interstate commerce exclusively federal or instead is it a concurrent state and federal power or is it instead a power of the several states, only?

Answer: The power to regulate interstate commerce is exclusively granted to the federal government in the United States. This power is derived from the Commerce Clause of the U.S. Constitution, which is found in Article I, Section 8, Clause 3.

The Commerce Clause grants Congress the authority to regulate commerce among the states. This authority has been interpreted broadly by the Supreme Court, allowing the federal government to regulate a wide range of activities that have an impact on interstate commerce, including not only the movement of goods and services across state lines but also activities that have a substantial effect on interstate commerce.

The Supreme Court has acknowledged that the power to regulate interstate commerce is exclusive to the federal government and cannot be exercised by individual states. This principle is known as the doctrine of federal preemption, which means that when Congress validly exercises its authority to regulate interstate commerce, its laws supersede conflicting state laws in that area.

Relevant Supreme Court cases regarding the federal government's exclusive power to regulate interstate commerce:

1. Gibbons v. Ogden, 22 U.S. (9 Wheat.) 1 (1824): This landmark case established the broad scope of the federal government's power to regulate interstate commerce. The Court held that the Commerce Clause grants Congress the authority to regulate not only the actual buying and selling of goods but also all aspects of commercial

intercourse that cross state lines. The case involved a dispute over a steamboat monopoly in New York and affirmed the federal government's supremacy in regulating interstate commerce. DEFINES COMMERCE

2. Wickard v. Filburn, 317 U.S. 111 (1942): In this influential case, the Supreme Court upheld the federal government's power to regulate purely local agricultural activity that had a substantial effect on interstate commerce. The Court held that even if an activity is local and non-commercial, if it has a substantial economic impact on interstate commerce, Congress can regulate it under the Commerce Clause. The case involved a farmer who exceeded his federally imposed wheat production quota for personal consumption. INTERSTATE COMMERCE INCLUDES IN STATE PRODUCTION AND CONSUMPTION WHICH AFFECTS INTERSTATE COMMERCE

What is meant by the term "dormant commerce clause"?

Answer: The "dormant commerce clause" is the implicit restriction on state legislation that interferes with or burdens interstate commerce, even in the absence of explicit federal regulation. It arises from the Commerce Clause of the United States Constitution which grants the federation exclusive power to regulate interstate commerce. When a state law affects interstate commerce it may be a violation of this division of powers and if it does it must be struck as unconstitutional. This is referred to as "the dormant commerce clause": it is the idea that there are implicit restrictions on states' power whenever the state's actions affect interstate commerce.

Relevant Case Citation: Pike v. Bruce Church, Inc., 397 U.S. 137 (1970) . Facts: Arizona statute required cantaloupes grown in the state to be packed in containers bearing the Arizona state mark. Bruce Church, Inc., a California-based company, challenged the law, arguing it violated the Commerce Clause by imposing an unreasonable burden on interstate commerce. Held: states have the authority to regulate intrastate commerce, but must not impose burdens on interstate commerce that exceed their legitimate local interests. The Court established the Pike balancing test, which requires courts to assess whether a state regulation discriminates against interstate commerce and, if so, whether the burden imposed on interstate commerce is outweighed by the local benefits of the regulation. Under Pike, a state law that discriminates against interstate commerce will be held unconstitutional unless the burden it imposes is justified by a legitimate local purpose and the burden on interstate commerce is not excessive in relation to the local benefits.

Keywords: Dormant commerce clause, Commerce Clause, Restrict state legislation, Interstate commerce

Exam Tip: When discussing the dormant commerce clause, analyze its purpose, the limitations it imposes on state legislation, and the balance between state and federal authority. Be prepared to apply the balancing test established by Pike v. Bruce Church, Inc. to assess whether a state law violates the dormant commerce clause.

Under what circumstances does a state law violate the dormant commerce clause?

Answer: A state law violates the dormant commerce clause when it discriminates against or treats in-state and out-of-state economic interests differently. The dormant commerce clause prohibits states from enacting laws that unduly burden or discriminate against interstate commerce, ensuring that economic activities between states are not hindered by protectionist measures.

Relevant Case Citation: Granholm v. Heald, 544 U.S. 460 (2005). Constitutionality of laws regulating the direct shipment of wine from out-of-state wineries to consumers; interpretation of dormant Commerce Clause and Twenty-first Amendment. Facts: Michigan and New York that allowed in-state wineries to directly ship wine to consumers but prohibited out-of-state wineries from doing the same. Plaintiffs, including wineries and consumers, argued that these laws violated the dormant Commerce Clause by discriminating against interstate commerce. Held: the state laws were unconstitutional. They discriminated against out-of-state wineries and imposed excessive burdens on interstate commerce. The Commerce Clause prohibits protectionist state regulations that favor in-state economic interests at the expense of out-of-state competitors. The Court rejected the argument that the laws were justified under the Twenty-first Amendment, which grants states broad authority to regulate the transportation and importation of alcoholic beverages. The Court clarified that while the Twenty-first Amendment grants states significant power over alcohol regulation, it must be interpreted consistently with other provisions of the Constitution.

Exam Tip: The "dormant" commerce clause is a fairly fine point of law and testable because it raises questions of the definitions of "commerce", "interstate", "regulate", as well as the division of powers between the federation and the states; exclusive versus concurrent powers, and thus can lead to supremacy clause issues. Study Granholm v. Heald and read the cases it cites to gain insight into the relevant legal principles. When discussing violations of the dormant commerce clause, analyze whether the state law discriminates against out-of-state economic interests, creates an undue burden on interstate commerce, or provides an advantage to in-state economic actors. Additionally, consider the balancing tests, such as the Pike v. Bruce Church, Inc. test, that courts may apply to determine the constitutionality of a state law under the dormant commerce clause. DCC issues are likelier to be tested by an essay question because there are many points over which one could argue! The law here is sufficiently settled that it can also be tested with a multiple choice question so do understand the positive law as well as the competing arguments, which mostly are about the definitions of commerce, interstate, regulate, affect.

In what two ways can a law violate the commerce clause?

Answer: A law can violate the commerce clause in two ways:

1. Expressly (facial): This occurs when a law explicitly treats in-state and out-of-state economic interests differently. The law's explicit language create disparate treatment based on the origin or location of economic activities. "Does just what it says on the tin."

2. Implicitly: This occurs when a law, although not expressly discriminatory, has the practical effect of treating in-state and out-of-state economic interests differently. It considers the impact or result of the law, regardless of the absence of explicit discriminatory language.

Relevant Case Citation: West Lynn Creamery, Inc. v. Healy, 512 U.S. 186 (1994). Challenge to a Massachusetts law that imposed a fee on milk dealers who purchased milk from out-of-state dairy farmers. The fee was intended to support a state milk promotion program. Issue: whether the Massachusetts law violated the dormant Commerce Clause of the United States Constitution, which prohibits states from enacting laws that discriminate against or unduly burden interstate commerce. Held: the Massachusetts law violated the dormant Commerce Clause. The law discriminated against out-of-state dairy farmers by imposing a disproportionate burden on their interstate commerce activities. The Court applied the Pike balancing test (supra in earlier questions), which requires weighing the burden on interstate commerce against the local benefits of the regulation. In this case, the Court found that the burden imposed on out-of-state dairy farmers outweighed any legitimate local benefits that Massachusetts sought to achieve through the fee.

Exam Insight: When discussing violations of the commerce clause, analyze whether the law explicitly treats in-state and out-of-state interests differently or if the practical effect of the law results in disparate treatment. Additionally, be prepared to apply the appropriate standard of review, such as strict scrutiny or the Pike balancing test, depending on the type of violation alleged under the commerce clause. Strict scrutiny applies to fundamental rights and suspect classes. Does the law inhibit a fundamental individual right? Or instead is it "merely" a conflict between two sovereigns *Powers* as opposed to and Individual's *Rights*? Conflicts between powers do not implicate concerns with destruction of individuals livelihoods and liberties by State Power and are thus not subject to strict scrutiny (compelling state interest, least restrictive means). The State has infinite means of oppression, but individuals have few means of resistance, which is *why* there is strict scrutiny.

What is the balancing test used to evaluate the dormant commerce clause?

Answer: The balance test used to evaluate the dormant commerce clause is the balancing of interests between the burden on interstate commerce and the value of the law to local interests. This test assesses whether the burden placed on interstate commerce by a particular state law is outweighed by the local benefits or interests that the law seeks to promote.

Relevant Case Citation: Pike v. Bruce Church, Inc., 397 U.S. 137 (1970) . See supra.

Mnemonic: To remember this concept, use the mnemonic: BBB Balance Burden Benefit ICC Local.

Exam Insight: Understanding the balance test applied to the dormant commerce clause: Familiarize yourself with cases like Pike v. Bruce Church, Inc. to gain insight into the relevant legal principles. When discussing the balancing test, analyze both the burden on interstate commerce and the local interests served by the law, and determine whether the burden outweighs the local benefits. Remember, if the burden on interstate commerce is excessive compared to the local interest, the law would be deemed unconstitutional under the dormant commerce clause. Link facts from the question to the rule to show *why* the balance tips as you conclude.

When is the dormant commerce clause balancing test applied?

Answer: The dormant commerce clause balancing test is applied when a law does not clearly discriminate against interstate commerce but incidentally burdens it. In such cases, the balancing test is used to evaluate whether the burden placed on interstate commerce is outweighed by the local benefits or interests that the law seeks to promote. If the State's burden on interstate commerce outweighs whatever legitimate benefit the state law seeks then the state law is unconstitutional due to a violation of the federation's exclusive power to regulate interstate commerce.

Relevant Case Citation: Maine v. Taylor, 477 U.S. 131 (1986) (State prohibited import of bait fish to prevent parasites and invasive species from destroying domestic fish. Constitutionally permissible: "The Maine statute is constitutional. The federal statute under which appellee was convicted did not waive the requirement of *Hughes v. Oklahoma*, 441 U. S. 322, that where a state statute, such as Maine's import ban, discriminates against interstate commerce either on its face or in practical effect, the State must show both that the statute serves a legitimate local purpose, and that this purpose cannot be served as well by available nondiscriminatory means. But the evidence amply supports the District Court's findings that Maine has made both showings."(syllabus))

Memorization Mnemonic: BBB Balance Burden Benefit IC>Local BBBICL. Visual: big blue bicycle balancing carefully between local and interstate concerns.

What is the standard of review for controversies involving aliens as a class?

Answer: The standard of review for controversies involving aliens as a class depends on whether the action is taken by the state or federal government.

For States' Actions: Strict scrutiny is applied, meaning the law or action must serve a compelling government interest and be narrowly tailored to achieve that interest. However, there is an exception when an important government job is involved, in which case rational basis review is applied. Under rational basis review, the law or action must be rationally related to a legitimate government interest.

For the Federation: Only rational basis review is applied. This means that the law or action must be rationally related to a legitimate government interest. The differing standards of review are justified by the Federation's exclusive foreign policy competence.

Relevant Case Citation: Graham v. Richardson, 403 U.S. 365 (1971): State laws that denied welfare benefits to legal resident aliens. Resident aliens in Arizona and Pennsylvania were denied state welfare benefits solely because they were not United States citizens. Held: these state laws violated the Equal Protection Clause of the Fourteenth Amendment to the United States Constitution. Unlawfully discriminated against aliens based on their alienage status, without any valid justification or compelling state interest. Equal Protection Clause requires a state to demonstrate a substantial reason for treating aliens differently from citizens in matters of public welfare.

Exam Insight: Remember that strict scrutiny requires a compelling government interest and narrow tailoring, while rational basis review only requires a rational relationship to a legitimate government interest.

Is it permissible for a private citizen to sue a state in federal court?

Answer: No, it is generally not permissible for a private citizen to sue a state in federal court. This limitation is imposed by the 11th Amendment to the United States Constitution, which grants states immunity from being sued by private individuals in federal court.

Relevant Case Citation: Hans v. Louisiana, 134 U.S. 1 (1890). Sovereign immunity. Issue: whether a citizen can sue their own state in federal court. Hans filed a lawsuit in federal court against Louisiana to challenge certain state bonds. He argued that the state's issuance of the bonds violated the Contracts Clause of the United States Constitution. Louisiana claimed immunity from the suit based on the principle of sovereign immunity, which shields states from being sued in federal court without their consent.

Held: a citizen cannot sue their own state in federal court (Eleventh Amendment). States enjoy immunity from being sued in federal court by their own citizens, absent their consent or certain exceptions not applicable in this case.

Can a member of a sovereign Native American tribe sue a state in federal court?

Answer: No, a member of a sovereign Native American tribe is generally not allowed to sue a state in federal court. Despite the sovereign status of Native American tribes, individual tribal members are still considered private citizens for the purpose of suing a state.

Relevant Case Citation: Kiowa Tribe of Oklahoma v. Manufacturing Technologies, Inc., 523 U.S. 751 (1998). Issue: whether the Kiowa Tribe could assert its sovereign immunity as a defense against a breach of contract claim brought by Manufacturing Technologies, Inc. (MTI), Facts: The dispute arose when the Tribe entered into a contract with MTI for the purchase of manufacturing equipment. The contract contained a forum selection clause that designated the state courts of Oklahoma as the exclusive jurisdiction for any disputes arising from the agreement. When a dispute over payment arose, MTI filed a lawsuit in an Oklahoma state court seeking damages for breach of contract. Kiowa Tribe argued that it was immune from suit under the doctrine of sovereign immunity. Held: tribal sovereign immunity barred suits against Indian tribes, even in the context of commercial activities. Sovereign immunity is a fundamental attribute of tribal sovereignty, as had been recognized in previous cases. Congress had not explicitly abrogated tribal sovereign immunity in the context of commercial contracts. Court rejected MTI's argument that the Tribe had waived its immunity by agreeing to the forum selection clause in the contract. Sovereign immunity could only be waived by clear and unequivocal language, and the forum selection clause did not meet that standard. Tribe held immune from suit and that the case could not proceed in the Oklahoma state court.

Exam Insight: Despite the sovereign status of Native American tribes, individual tribal members are still treated as private citizens and generally cannot sue states in federal court. However, tribes themselves have sovereign immunity: exceptionally, an Indian Tribe may be able to sue a State in Federal court or, likelier may sue the Federation to compel a remedy when that Indian Tribe is injured by one of the several States. This is because of the principle that the Federation is the sole authority for dealing with other Nations, including "Domestic Dependent Nations".

Can the state of New York sue the state of California in federal court?

Answer: Yes, the state of New York can sue the state of California in federal court. States have the ability to sue other states in federal court under certain circumstances.

Citation: Article III, Section 2, Clause 1 of the U.S. Constitution:

"The judicial Power shall extend to all Cases, in Law and Equity, arising under this Constitution, the Laws of the United States, and Treaties made, or which shall be made, under their Authority;—to all Cases affecting Ambassadors, other public Ministers and Consuls;—to all Cases of admiralty and maritime Jurisdiction;—to Controversies to which the United States shall be a Party;—to Controversies between two or more States..."

This quote from Article III, Section 2, Clause 1 of the U.S. Constitution explicitly states that the judicial power extends to controversies between two or more states. Therefore, the state of New York can indeed sue the state of California in federal court if a controversy arises between them.

Is it permissible for a foreign government to sue a U.S. state in federal court?

Answer: No, it is generally not permissible for a foreign government to sue a U.S. state in federal court. This is consistent with the general rule that Indian Tribes cannot sue one of the several states. The 11th Amendment of the United States Constitution prohibits foreign nations from suing U.S. states in federal court. This is because of the U.S. Federation's exclusive foreign policy competence. Thus, a foreign State, i.e. another country, to seek a legal remedy in court against one of the states, must proceed against the Federation, not the State.

Relevant Case Citation: Principality of Monaco v. Mississippi, 292 U.S. 313 (1934)

Memorization Mnemonic: 11 NOFOR

Does the U.S. President have the authority to decline to spend funds that were appropriated by Congress for a particular purpose?

Answer: No, the U.S. President does not have the authority to decline to spend funds that were appropriated by Congress for a particular purpose. The President has the duty to ensure that the laws are "faithfully executed," which includes the obligation to implement the appropriations made by Congress.

Relevant Case Citation: Train v. City of New York, 420 U.S. 35 (1975). City of New York challenged the constitutionality of certain provisions of the Federal-Aid Highway Act, arguing that they violated the Tenth Amendment of the United States Constitution. The provisions in question required states to adopt certain highway safety standards in order to receive federal funding; upheld the constitutionality of the provisions and ruled in favor of the Secretary of Transportation. The Court held that the federal government had the authority to condition the receipt of federal funds on compliance with certain regulations and standards.

Memorization Mnemonic: Did you ever hear about the end of the year spending rush by the administrative agencies? Their tendency to be sure to have spent all remaining allocated funds prior to the end of their fiscal year? That political fact may be a reflection of this legal rule, which requires the president to have spent those funds allocated to his administration by congress.

Exam Insight: When discussing the President's authority to spend funds, explain that the President does not have the discretion to decline spending funds that have been appropriated by Congress for a particular purpose. The President's duty to faithfully execute the laws includes the obligation to implement the appropriations made by Congress. Remember to analyze the limitations on the President's authority, such as the Anti-Deficiency Act, which prohibits the President from spending funds in excess of the amounts appropriated by Congress.

What types of laws may be passed under the 13th Amendment?

Answer: Under the 13th Amendment to the United States Constitution, the following types of laws may be passed: (1) Laws that prevent public or private entities from furthering slavery or indentured servitude. This includes laws aimed at eradicating and prohibiting any form of coerced labor or involuntary servitude.

(2) The Supreme Court of the United States (SCOTUS) has held that laws that promotes a badge of slavery or any incident to slavery are unconstitutional, even if the law is addresses private rights and not the public power. This means that laws cannot perpetuate or support practices that are reminiscent of slavery or that enable conditions similar to slavery. One cannot indenture themselves under current law.

Relevant Case Citation: United States v. Kozminski, 487 U.S. 931 (1988). Facts: Prosecution against Joseph Kozminski for violating a federal statute that prohibited the involuntary servitude of another person. Kozminski was the owner and operator of a residential care facility for mentally ill individuals in Michigan, accused of subjecting residents to physical and psychological abuse, essentially forcing them into involuntary servitude. Issue: was evidence presented sufficient to establish Kozminski violated the federal statute, that definedinvoluntary servitude as a condition where a person is held against their will and compelled to work under threat of physical or legal coercion. Held: Evidence of the use of coercion or threats to force individuals to work against their will was sufficient to establish Kozminski had violated the federal statute prohibiting involuntary servitude. **Involuntary servitude extends beyond traditional forms of physical bondage and can include psychological coercion** and control. This broad interpretation of the statute aimed to protect individuals from all forms of forced labor and exploitation.

Exam Insight: When discussing the types of laws that may be passed under the 13th Amendment, explain that the amendment empowers Congress to enact laws that prohibit both public and private entities from furthering slavery or indentured servitude. Additionally, note that the Supreme Court has established that laws cannot allow conduct that promotes a badge of slavery or is incident to slavery, even when applied to private citizens. Remember to analyze the specific language and purpose of the 13th Amendment when assessing the constitutionality of laws related to slavery and involuntary servitude.

Under what circumstances does a government worker have a property right in their position?

Answer: A government worker has a property right in their position when they can only be removed for cause. In such cases, the government worker is entitled to certain due process protections before their employment can be terminated.

Relevant Case Citation: Cleveland Board of Education v. Loudermill, 470 U.S. 532 (1985). Due process rights of public employees facing termination or disciplinary action. Facts: Loudermill, a Cleveland public school employee was fired; argued his termination violated his constitutional right to due process under the Fourteenth Amendment. Issue: was Loudermill entitled to a pre-termination hearing? (due process) Cleveland Board of Education argued that Loudermill's termination was justified based on the nature of his position and the evidence against him, and that a post-termination hearing was sufficient to satisfy due process requirements. Held: Loudermill was entitled to a pre-termination hearing. Public employees have a property interest in continued employment. Deprivation of this interest without adequate procedural safeguards would violate due process. Two-step process for determining required procedural protections. First, Before a public employee can be terminated, they are entitled to notice of the charges against them and an opportunity to respond. This pre-termination hearing should provide the employee with an opportunity to present their side of the story and contest the evidence or reasons for termination. Second, pre-termination hearing does not need to be an elaborate or formal process but should be a meaningful opportunity for the employee to be heard and address the allegations against them. The specific procedures for the pre-termination hearing may vary depending on the circumstances, but some level of notice and an opportunity to respond must be provided.

Exam Insight: When discussing government workers' property rights, explain that a property right arises when a government worker can only be removed for cause, meaning there must be a valid reason or grounds for termination. Note that this entitles the worker to certain due process protections before their employment can be terminated. Analyze the specific factors and standards established in relevant case law, such as the Loudermill case, when determining the existence and extent of a government worker's property right.

If a government worker has a property right in their position, what must they be afforded before termination?

Answer: If a government worker has a property right in their position (= can only be fired "for cause"), they must be afforded the following before termination:

(1) Notice of the charges against them, providing information about the allegations or reasons for termination.

(2) The basis or reason for termination must be communicated to the worker, ensuring transparency and clarity regarding the grounds for their potential dismissal.

(3) The worker must be given an opportunity to be heard, which includes the right to respond to the charges and present their case in front of a neutral adjudicator.

Relevant Case Citation: Board of Regents of State Colleges v. Roth, 408 U.S. 564 (1972). Constitutional rights of non-tenured public employees in the context of their employment termination. Facts: Roth was employed as a nontenured instructor at a state college in Wisconsin. Roth's contract was not renewed after his first year of employment. He sued the Board of Regents, claiming termination violated his constitutional rights. Issue: whether Roth had a constitutionally protected property interest in his continued employment, which would entitle him to due process protections under the Fourteenth Amendment. Held: Roth did not have a constitutionally protected property interest in his employment. The Court concluded that nontenured public employees do not have a legitimate expectation of continued employment, as their employment is typically of a temporary or probationary nature. A property interest in continued employment arises only when there is a legitimate claim of entitlement created by contract, statute, or other mutually explicit understanding. In the absence of such an entitlement, a nontenured employee's termination does not implicate due process concerns.

Memorization Trick: NO HERD; NBO. Notice Opportunity to be Heard. Imagine a herd of icecream bunnies on the Base. What an OPPORTUNITY! Based or baseless? There is NO such ThIng as ICE bunnies let alone a herd of them!

Exam Insight: Understanding the procedural protections required for government workers with a property right in their position is important for constitutional law exams. To remember this concept, use the mnemonic NBO (Notice, Basis, Opportunity). Familiarize yourself with cases like Board of Regents of State Colleges v. Roth to gain insight into the relevant legal principles. When discussing the rights of government workers, explain that if a worker has a property right in their position, they are entitled to procedural due process before termination. This includes receiving notice of the charges, being informed of the basis for termination, and having an opportunity to be heard in front of a neutral adjudicator. Analyze the specific requirements and standards established in relevant case law, such as the Roth case, to assess the adequacy of the procedural protections afforded to government workers.

What are the requirements for regulating commercial speech?

Answer: The requirements for regulating commercial speech are as follows:

(1) The law must further a substantial government interest.

(2) The regulation must actually advance or further that government interest.

(3) The law must be narrowly tailored, meaning it should not burden more speech than necessary to achieve its intended purpose.

Relevant Case Citation: Central Hudson Gas & Electric Corp. v. Public Service Commission, 447 U.S. 557 (1980). Regulation of commercial speech and addressed the constitutionality of restrictions on advertising by public utilities. New York Public Service Commission (PSC) issued regulations that prohibited certain types of advertising by electric utilities, including promotional advertising that encouraged the use of electricity. Central Hudson Gas & Electric Corp., an electric utility, challenged the regulations, arguing that they violated its First Amendment rights. Issue: whether the PSC's regulations violated the First Amendment's protection of commercial speech. Four-part test to determine the constitutionality of the regulations:

First, whether the speech was protected commercial speech. Commercial speech is speech that proposes a commercial transaction or relates to the economic interests of the speaker and the audience. The Court held that the advertising in question constituted protected commercial speech.

Second, whether the government had a substantial interest in regulating the speech. In this case, the Court recognized that the government's interest in conserving energy and promoting energy efficiency was substantial.

Third, whether the regulations directly advanced the government's substantial interest. Although the regulations partially advanced the government's interest, they also imposed a complete ban on certain types of speech, which was more extensive than necessary.

Finally, whether the regulations were narrowly tailored to achieve the government's interest. The Court held that the regulations were not sufficiently narrowly tailored because they prohibited more speech than necessary to achieve the government's goals.

Held: PSC's regulations violated the First Amendment.

The Central Hudson test for evaluating restrictions on commercial speech requires that the government show a substantial interest, that the regulation directly advances that interest, and that the regulation is narrowly tailored. A substantial interest (intermediate scrutiny) is less important than a compelling state interest (strict scrutiny). This is a point over which one could argue on an essay and gain points by a persuasive well structured argument, which is the key to performing exceptionally well on essay exams.

Memorization Trick: SiN Gov, advance narrow tailor (substantial interest of the government). Visualization:Slenderman wants to sell you deadly instrumentalities! He's on a tv commercial advertisement. In Slenderman's commercial he is wearing a Narrowly Tailored suit, but the sinful government uses his knives to cut some tape, and then tapes his mouth shut, to stop his murder spree. Sin gov, advance narrow tailor.

Exam Insight: When discussing the requirements for regulating commercial speech, explain that regulations must meet the Central Hudson test, which includes showing a substantial government interest, actual advancement of that interest, and a narrow tailoring of the regulation. Analyze the specific factors and standards established in relevant case law, such as the Central Hudson case, when evaluating the constitutionality of regulations on commercial speech. You may have the opportunity to compare intermediate scrutiny with strict scrutiny and rational review, but only raise arguments in the alternative where they are relevant to answering the question asked. Answer the question asked, but part of your answer should be making persuasive structured arguments, possibly even about what the law is in areas where the law is not settled.

What is obscenity?

Answer: Obscenity is the depiction or description of sexual conduct that meets the following criteria:

(1) It appeals to a prurient interest in sex, it stimulates or arouses an unhealthy or morbid curiosity about sexual matters.

(2) It portrays sex in a "patently" offensive manner, where the material goes beyond mere offensiveness and is clearly and obviously offensive in its sexual content.

(3) It lacks any redeeming artistic, literary, political, scientific, or social value. In other words, it has no recognized merit in areas such as art, literature, politics, science, or society. Who exactly judges what has "artistic value"?

Relevant Case Citation: Miller v. California, 413 U.S. 15 (1973). Facts: Miller was convicted under California law for distributing obscene materials. Issue: constitutional standards for obscenity. The three parts of the Miller test are as follows: 1. The average person, applying contemporary community standards, would find that the work, taken as a whole, appeals to the prurient interest. I guess prurient means "sex", maybe bloodshed? I have no idea... AND 2. The work depicts or describes sexual conduct in a patently offensive way, specifically defined by state law. AND 3. The work, taken as a whole, lacks serious literary, artistic, political, or scientific value. Pretty much any work can be argued to have some sort of artistic value. This test is lame. All three prongs must be met. So now we live in a society where trash talk is completely normal and children get porn. Congratulations?

Memorization Mnemonic: Sexy Prurient butt Offensive ASP (artistic, scientific, social, political) is not obscene because of its artistic value.

Exam Tips: Obscenity involves sexual depictions or descriptions that appeal to a prurient interest, are patently offensive, and lack any recognized artistic, literary, political, scientific, or social value. Obscenity is not protected by the First Amendment and can be regulated by states but is so narrowly defined as to be irrelevant. Obviously there is enormous space on this issue for coherent rational well-founded argument on an essay. So this is likelier to be the object of an essay than of a multiple choice quesiton. Analyze the specific factors and tests established in relevant case law, such as the Miller test, when assessing whether material meets the standard of obscenity. Remember to consider community standards and contemporary societal values when applying the obscenity standard.

Is a state government permitted to impose restrictions on obscenity?

Answer: Yes, a state government is allowed to impose restrictions on obscenity. Obscenity is not protected speech under the First Amendment of the United States Constitution.

Relevant Case Citation: Miller v. California, 413 U.S. 15 (1973) (see prior question's answer)

Memotechnique: Prurient Puritans May Flower or Deflower when confronting Jaded Cynics.

Exam Insight: Familiarize yourself with cases like Miller v. California to gain insight into the relevant legal principles. When discussing obscenity, explain that it falls outside the scope of protected speech under the First Amendment. Therefore, state governments have the authority to enforce restrictions on obscenity. Analyze the specific factors and tests established in relevant case law, such as the Miller test, when assessing whether material qualifies as obscene. Remember to consider the community standards and contemporary societal values when determining the constitutionality of state restrictions on obscenity. That which is obscene depends somewhat on the social context, something shocking and obviously rude in a rustic rural region might be met with blasé indifference in a jaded urban community full of lawless cynics. Or, if you prefer, puritans may more readily find things prurient. "Would you show this to a literal child?" seems like the only sensible standard.

If a treaty between the United States and another country conflicts with a state law, is the U.S. President authorized to declare the state law invalid?

Answer: Yes, the U.S. President has the authority to declare a state law invalid if it conflicts with a treaty between the United States and another country. This power is derived from Article 2, Section 2, Clause 2 of the United States Constitution, also known as the Supremacy Clause. According to the Supremacy Clause, treaties are considered the supreme law of the land, and any state law that contradicts a valid treaty is rendered invalid.

Relevant Case Citation: Missouri v. Holland, 252 U.S. 416 (1920). If you are interested in international law this is a must-read case. State sovereignty versus federal power re: international treaties. Missouri challenged the federal government's authority to regulate hunting of migratory birds. Issue: whether a treaty could empower the federal government to enact legislation that would otherwise exceed the scope of its constitutional authority. USA had entered into a treaty, the Migratory Bird Treaty Act, with Great Britain, to protect migratory birds that crossed international borders. Pursuant to the treaty, the federal government passed a law prohibiting the hunting of migratory birds. Missouri argued the federal regulation infringed on the state's sovereign rights to regulate wildlife within its borders. The state contended that the federal government's authority was limited to the powers explicitly granted by the Constitution and that the regulation of wildlife fell under the state's reserved powers. Federal government's authority to regulate the hunting of migratory birds under the Migratory Bird Treaty Act upheld. Treaty power granted to the federal government by the Constitution allows Congress to enact legislation that would otherwise exceed its constitutional authority, as long as the treaty is a valid exercise of federal power. Federation can indeed arrogate power via international treaty from the states. Most likely such arrogation would only be lawful where the treaty is ratified by the Senate, one may argue that point.

The Supremacy Clause of the US Constitution makes treaties "the supreme law of the land,". When a treaty is validly formed (ratified), it can constitutionally override conflicting state laws. The federal government's treaty power not limited by the reserved powers of the states. Federal government's authority to enter into and implement valid treaties can expand its powers beyond those enumerated in the Constitution. This case affirmed the supremacy of federal law over conflicting state laws in matters involving international treaties.

Memorization Mnemonic: Missouri Migratory Holland International Treaty Power Prerogative Power Arrogate from States MM HIT PPP AS

Exam Insight: Understanding the relationship between treaties, state laws, and the Supremacy Clause is important for constitutional law exams. To remember this concept, use the mnemonic. Read Missouri v. Holland and cases citing it and cited therein to gain insight into the relevant legal principles. When discussing the authority of the President to invalidate state laws, explain that the Supremacy Clause establishes that treaties are the supreme law of the land. Therefore, if a state law conflicts with a treaty, the President has the power to declare the state law invalid. Analyze the specific factors and standards established in relevant case law, such as the Missouri v. Holland case, when determining the constitutionality of conflicts between treaties and state laws. Remember to consider the interplay of federal and state powers when assessing the validity of state laws in light of treaty obligations.

Define: substantive due process

Answer: Substantive due process is a legal principle derived from the Due Process Clause of the Fourteenth Amendment. The Due Process Clause provides that no state shall "deprive any person of life, liberty, or property without due process of law."

Substantive due process is the concept that certain fundamental rights are protected from government interference, even if there are procedural safeguards in place. In other words, it recognizes that the government's actions must not only comply with fair procedures but must also be based on a legitimate and justifiable purpose.

Under substantive due process, courts examine whether a law or government action infringes upon fundamental rights or liberties. These rights are not explicitly listed in the Constitution but have been recognized by the courts as essential to the concept of ordered liberty. Examples of such rights include the right to privacy, freedom of speech, freedom of religion, and the right to marry.

To determine whether a law violates substantive due process, courts typically apply different levels of scrutiny. Strict scrutiny is applied when a fundamental right is involved, requiring the government to demonstrate a compelling interest and that the law is narrowly tailored to achieve that interest. Intermediate scrutiny is applied when the law affects a right that is important but not fundamental, and a rational basis test is used for laws that do not implicate fundamental rights.

It's important to note that substantive due process has been the subject of ongoing legal debate and interpretation. The scope and application of substantive due process have evolved over time through court decisions, and its precise boundaries continue to be a matter of discussion and interpretation in the legal community.

Exam Tip: Because of its self-contradictory nature and consequent controverted character "substantive due process" would be likelier to be tested in an essay question rather than a multiple choice question. There's lots of room for argument but in fact "procedure" and "substance" are opposite concepts, the "how to" and "what is" of law. Consequently the idea of substantive content to due process is an illogical self-contradiction and in my view ultimately untenable.

What does procedural due process guarantee?

Answer: Procedural due process guarantees the following:

(1) Notice: Individuals must be provided with adequate notice regarding the charges or actions being taken against them, ensuring they have knowledge of the allegations or reasons for the potential deprivation of their rights.

(2) An opportunity to be heard: Individuals must be afforded the opportunity to present their side of the case, respond to the charges or actions, and provide evidence or arguments in their defense.

(3) A neutral adjudicator: The proceedings must be conducted before an impartial and unbiased decision-maker or adjudicator who will objectively evaluate the facts and arguments presented.

Relevant Case Citation: Goldberg v. Kelly, 397 U.S. 254 (1970). Due process rights of welfare recipients facing termination of their benefits. Issue: whether due process clause of the Fourteenth Amendment required a pre-termination evidentiary hearing for welfare recipients before the termination of their benefits. The plaintiffs argued that the termination of benefits without a prior hearing violated their constitutional rights to notice and an opportunity to be heard. Held: welfare recipients have a right to a pre-termination evidentiary hearing before their benefits can be terminated. Welfare benefits are a form of "property" protected by the Due Process Clause, and therefore, individuals have a constitutionally protected interest in continued receipt of those benefits. Welfare benefits are often essential for recipients' survival and well-being, and their termination without due process could have severe consequences. Consequently, the Court concluded that prior notice and an opportunity to present their case in a hearing were necessary to protect recipients from erroneous or arbitrary terminations. Recipients must be given timely and adequate notice of the reasons for the proposed termination, an opportunity to review the evidence against them, an opportunity to present their side of the case, and the right to be represented by counsel or an authorized representative.

Memorization Mnemonic: NOAh's ark had plenty of food (Notice, Opportunity, Adjudicator)

Exam Insight: Understanding the guarantees of procedural due process is essential for constitutional law exams. To remember this concept, use the mnemonic NOA (Notice, Opportunity, Adjudicator). Familiarize yourself with cases like Goldberg v. Kelly to gain insight into the relevant legal principles. When discussing procedural due process, explain that it ensures individuals are provided with notice, an opportunity to be heard, and a neutral adjudicator. Analyze the specific requirements and standards established in relevant case law, such as the Goldberg case, when assessing whether procedural due process has been respected in a given situation. Remember to consider the balance between individual rights and the government's interests when evaluating the adequacy of procedural safeguards.

What does substantive due process guarantee?

Answer: Substantive due process guarantees that laws will be reasonable and not arbitrary. It ensures that government actions and laws do not infringe upon fundamental rights in a manner that lacks a legitimate purpose or justification. In truth it is the fundamental right ("inalienable rights") which is being upheld. Although the Declaration of Independence, as a "mere" declartion of political intent is but hortatory, a hortatory instrument such as the declaration or the preamble has persuasive value ("ought") as evidence of law, for customary common law is "only" that which is done (usages) under the believe that such be lawful (opinio) (whether commanded, permitted, or prohibited). Fundamental ("inalienable") rights are inherent to any person, whereas civil and political rights are conditioned on citizenship or at least residency. Upon liberation, all former slaves were accorded a right to U.S. citizenship, which is why the fight for equal justice under law is called, somewhat inaccurately, the "civil rights" movement, for the fundamental rights are both more essential and more broadly enjoyed than civil rights (rights of citizens) or political rights (which may not have legal force despite political power).

Keywords "inalienable right" "fundamental right" "arbitrary" "capricious" "abuse of discretion"

Memorization Mnemonic: RAL (Reasonable, Arbitrary, Legitimate)

Exam Insight: Understanding the concept of substantive due process is important for constitutional law exams. To remember this concept, use the mnemonic RAL (Reasonable, Arbitrary, Legitimate). Familiarize yourself with cases like Roe v. Wade to gain insight into the relevant legal principles. When discussing substantive due process, explain that it guarantees that laws and government actions must be reasonable and not arbitrary. They should have a legitimate purpose or justification and should not infringe upon fundamental rights without proper justification. Analyze the specific factors and tests established in relevant case law, such as the balancing test used in Roe v. Wade, when determining whether a law violates substantive due process. Remember to consider the level of scrutiny applied to determine the constitutionality of the government action or law under substantive due process. Try to understand the distinctions between inalienable individual rights, collective rights, civil rights, and political rights, they are "the thread of Ariadne" (红线).

From which constitutional clause is substantive due process protection derived? Include, if possible, specific text quoted from the relevant provisions of the U.S. Constitution.

Answer: Substantive due process protection is derived from the following constitutional clauses:

Federal: The Fifth Amendment of the United States Constitution, which states, "No person shall be... deprived of life, liberty, or property, without due process of law."

State: The Fourteenth Amendment of the United States Constitution, specifically the Due Process Clause, which states, "nor shall any State deprive any person of life, liberty, or property, without due process of law."

Exam Insight: When discussing substantive due process, explain that its protection is derived from the Fifth Amendment at the federal level and the Due Process Clause of the Fourteenth Amendment at the state level (Federal Fifth, 14 States). Analyze the specific factors and tests established in relevant case law, such as the undue burden standard set forth in Planned Parenthood v. Casey, when assessing whether a law violates substantive due process. Remember to consider the level of scrutiny applied and the fundamental rights implicated when evaluating the constitutionality of government actions or laws under substantive due process.

Name some landmark cases that shaped substantive due process

Answer: There have been several landmark cases in the United States that have shaped the concept of substantive due process. Here are a few notable examples:

1. Roe v. Wade (1973): This case dealt with a woman's constitutional right to privacy in relation to abortion. The Supreme Court held that a woman has a fundamental right under the Due Process Clause to choose to have an abortion, subject to certain limitations.

1. Planned Parenthood v. Casey (1992): In this case, the Supreme Court reaffirmed the central holding of Roe v. Wade and clarified the standard for evaluating restrictions on abortion. It established the "undue burden" test, which requires that any abortion regulation not place a substantial obstacle in the path of a woman seeking an abortion.

2. Lawrence v. Texas (2003): The Supreme Court struck down a Texas law that criminalized consensual same-sex sexual activity. The Court held that the law violated substantive due process and recognized a fundamental right to engage in private, consensual sexual conduct.

3. Obergefell v. Hodges (2015): This case addressed the issue of same-sex marriage. The Supreme Court held that the fundamental right to marry is guaranteed to same-sex couples under the Due Process and Equal Protection Clauses of the Fourteenth Amendment.

4. Griswold v. Connecticut (1965): The Supreme Court recognized a right to privacy in the context of marital relations and invalidated a Connecticut law that prohibited the use of contraceptives. Although the Court did not explicitly mention substantive due process, the decision laid the foundation for later cases.

Because these cases all concern unwritten, i.e. customary common law, the unwritten common law constitution over which the revolutionaries fought a years-long war against their sovereign, they are contentious for their extent is consequently uncertain, vague, and can often only be understood on a case-by-case basis. Partly they depend on how seriously we take historical and literal interpretations of law. They are excellent topics for essays, where one can make a structured coherent persuasive argument. They are less susceptible of multiple choice testing.

These cases illustrate how the concept of substantive due process has been applied to protect fundamental rights in various contexts, including reproductive rights, sexual privacy, and marriage equality. This list is not exhaustive, and there have been many other cases that have contributed to the development of substantive due process jurisprudence. They are all susceptible to judicial revision as the Court continues to move more toward literalist and historic interpretation and away from interpretivism, which has been the legal trend for at least 30 years.

What are some examples of fundamental rights?

Answer: Fundamental rights include:

(1) The right to procreate: This encompasses the freedom to make decisions regarding reproduction and family planning.

(2) The right to vote: This guarantees individuals the ability to participate in the democratic process by casting their votes in elections. Strictly speaking however this ought be seen as a civil or political right, since non-citizens do not enjoy the right to vote. They do however have political rights such as the right to public protest, possibly also the right to petition, since petition is a non-binding political remedy.

(3) The right to travel interstate: This ensures the freedom to move and travel between different states within the United States. This is one of the few rights protected by the privileges and immunities clause (PIC). If you see "the right to travel" on the bar exam it is almost certainly a PIC question. If you see the PIC invoked on the bar exam as an answer choice and the right to travel is NOT relevant to the question then that answer choice is likely wrong.

(4) The freedom of speech: This protects individuals' rights to express their opinions and ideas without unwarranted government interference. This is both a fundamental right (all people have it) and a political right (it may be used to form and express political willpower).

(5) The right to privacy: This includes the protection of personal autonomy and the ability to make private decisions without undue intrusion from the government.
Each of these can and should be linked to one of the amendments to the US Const. That bill of rights is not exhaustive! You may also wish to link your fundamental rights/SDP claim to the English Bill of

Rights, or even Magna Chart. Again, they fought a revolution to be able to legally enforce these very rights.

Relevant Case Citation: Griswold v. Connecticut, 381 U.S. 479 (1965).

Memorization Mnemonic: PP TVS (Privacy Procreate, Travel, Vote, Speech)

Exam Insight: Understanding fundamental rights is central for constitutional law exams. To remember this concept, use the mnemonic PP TVS (Privacy Procreate, Travel, Vote, Speech). Familiarize yourself with cases like Griswold v. Connecticut to gain insight into the relevant legal principles. When discussing fundamental rights, explain that they are protected by the Constitution and safeguard individual liberties. If you can usefully do so, distinguish "claims", "privileges", "rights", and "liberties" from each other. Analyze the specific rights and standards established in relevant case law, such as the right to privacy recognized in Griswold v. Connecticut, when assessing the constitutionality of government actions or laws. Remember to consider the level of scrutiny applied to determine the validity of laws affecting fundamental rights and the balancing of individual liberties with compelling government interests.

What is the limit on Congress's power to investigate and subpoena?

Answer: The limit on Congress's power to investigate and subpoena is that it may only exercise these powers on matters for which Congress has the power to legislate. This means that Congress cannot engage in investigations or issue subpoenas that exceed its legislative authority.

Relevant Case Citation: McGrain v. Daugherty, 273 U.S. 135 (1927). Fifth Amendment privilege against self-incrimination. Teapot Dome scandal, secret leasing of federal oil reserves (corruption). Senate established a committee to investigate. During the investigation, the committee sought to subpoena the Attorney General to testify and produce certain documents related to the scandal. Daugherty refused to comply, claiming it violated his Fifth Amendment privilege against self-incrimination. Senate then brought a lawsuit against Daugherty, seeking a court order to enforce the subpoena. Issue: whether the Senate had the authority to compel Daugherty's testimony and the production of documents.

Issue: "(a) whether the Senate-or the House of Representatives, both being on the same plane in this regard - has power, through its own process, to compel a private individual to appear before it or one of its committees and give testimony needed to enable it efficiently to exercise a legislative function belonging to it under the Constitution; and (b) whether it sufficiently appears that the process was being employed in this instance to obtain testimony for that purpose." https://openjurist.org/273/us/135

Held: Senate has the power to conduct investigations and compel witnesses to testify. The Court emphasized that the power of investigation is inherent in the legislative process and is essential to the proper functioning of the government. Fifth Amendment privilege against self-incrimination did not shield him from testifying before the committee or producing the requested documents. The privilege only applies to criminal proceedings and does not extend to legislative investigations.

Exam Insight: When discussing Congress's power to investigate and subpoena, explain that it is limited to matters on which Congress has the power to legislate: it is an auxiliary, implied power and exists to the extent necessary and proper for congress to be able to exercise its legal duties. Analyze the specific factors and tests established in relevant case law, such as the "necessary and proper" clause discussed in McGrain v. Daugherty, when assessing the constitutionality of congressional investigations and subpoenas. Remember to consider the separation of powers and the balance between Congress's investigatory authority and individual rights when evaluating the scope of congressional inquiries.

What conditions must be present for Congress to properly regulate state action through the spending power? That is, when and how may congress condition grants of funds to states?

Answer: For Congress to properly regulate state action through the spending power, the following conditions must be present:

(1) The conditions of federal funding are clearly stated: Congress must clearly specify the conditions attached to the receipt of federal funds, ensuring that states are aware of the obligations and requirements they must adhere to in order to receive the funding.

(2) The conditions relate to the purposes of the spending directly: The conditions imposed by Congress must have a direct relationship to the specific purposes for which the federal funds are being allocated. They should be logically connected to the intended goals and objectives of the spending program.

(3) The conditions and spending are not unduly coercive: Congress cannot employ conditions that unduly coerce states into compliance. The conditions must be reasonably related to the federal interest at stake and cannot be so coercive as to leave states with no real choice but to comply.

Relevant Case Citation: South Dakota v. Dole, 483 U.S. 203 (1987). Constitutionality of conditional federal funding for states. Congress passed a law that withheld a portion of federal highway funds from states that did not raise their legal drinking age to 21. South Dakota challenged the constitutionality of this condition, arguing it violated principles of federalism and exceeded Congress's spending power. Held: Congress has the authority to attach conditions to the receipt of federal funds as long as those conditions are reasonably related to the federal interest in the program.

The Court established a four-part test to determine the constitutionality of conditional spending. First, the spending must be for the general welfare. Second, the conditions must be unambiguous and relate to the federal interest in the program. Third, the conditions must be related to the federal interest in the program. Finally, the conditions must not be coercive, meaning that the states should have a genuine choice in accepting or rejecting the funds. The drinking age condition met all four criteria. It determined that the condition was reasonably related to the federal interest in promoting highway safety and reducing alcohol-related accidents among young drivers. Additionally, the Court held that the condition was not unduly coercive because the financial pressure on the states was not so great as to leave them with no real choice but to comply.

Memorization Mnemonics: Drunk Dakota Driver gets no Federal Dollars. See SS spends pence; CSSPNC (Clearly Stated, Specific Purposes, Not Coercive).

Exam Insight: The most famous example is highway funding. Congress issues grants and matching funds conditioned on state compliance and contributions. When discussing the conditions for proper regulation, explain that the conditions must be clearly stated in the federal funding, directly related to the purposes of the spending program, and not unduly coercive. Analyze the specific factors and tests established in relevant case law, such as the "relatively mild encouragement" test set forth in South Dakota v. Dole, when assessing the constitutionality of conditions imposed by Congress on state funding. Remember to consider the balance between federal and state powers and the potential impact on states' sovereignty when evaluating the conditions attached to federal funds. There are "lurking" issues of sovereignty (Federation and State are both sovereigns, alike in equal dignity) as well as "division of powers", perhaps also of concurrent powers. Could congress constitutionally use funding to empower or disempower the States to undertake or refrain from acting in an area of exclusive state competence? The ability to spot and argue persuasively about these "gray zone" "unsettled issues" can win points on essay exams and this topic is likelier to be tested by an essay rather than a multiple choice question (MCQ) for that reason, though the law is adequately settled that an MCQ on the topic would also be possible.

May a state tax a publication based on its content?

Answer: No, a state may generally not tax a publication based on its content. Taxes specifically targeting the content of publications are subject to strict scrutiny, which is a high standard to meet especially because the burden is on the government to prove the measure is strictly necessary to meet a compelling state interest. Taxes on speech would be viewed as seriously infringing on the First Amendment rights of freedom of speech and the press.

Publishers are however still subject to general business taxes that apply to all businesses operating within the state. These taxes are not based on the content of the publication but rather on the general business activities and revenues.

Relevant Case Citation: Minneapolis Star Tribune Co. v. Minnesota Commissioner of Revenue, 460 U.S. 575 (1983)

Minneapolis Star Tribune Co. v. Minnesota Commissioner of Revenue, 460 U.S. 575 (1983). First Amendment's *RIGHT* to freedom of the press versus taxation *POWER*. Newspaper publisher, challenged constitutionality of a Minnesota state tax that imposed a use tax on ink and paper used in the production of newspapers. The newspaper argued that the tax violated the First Amendment's protection of freedom of the press by singling out newspapers for taxation.

Held: tax on ink and paper used in the production of newspapers was unconstitutional under the First Amendment. The press plays a vital role in the dissemination of information, opinions, and ideas, and that any tax specifically targeting newspapers could potentially burden or chill the exercise of that freedom. Applied heightened standard of scrutiny known as "strict scrutiny" to analyze the tax. Under this standard, the government must demonstrate a compelling interest in imposing the tax and show that the tax is narrowly tailored to serve that interest. The state's interest in raising revenue was not a compelling enough reason to justify the tax on newspapers. It concluded that the tax singled out the press for special treatment and had the potential to inhibit the free flow of information and ideas.

Memorization Mnemonic: Tax Content? Strict Scrutiny! First, AM: Texas South & Carolina have Taxes and Strict Scrutiny. (first amendment taxation thereof = strict scrutiny).

What is the constitutional limit on public school punishments?

Answer: The constitutional limit on public school punishments is that a significant suspension, typically 10 days or longer, or a more severe punishment may not be imposed without providing the student with a hearing. Due process considerations require that students facing substantial disciplinary actions be afforded an opportunity to present their side of the story and defend themselves before the punishment is imposed.

Relevant Case Citation: Goss v. Lopez, 419 U.S. 565 (1975)

Several high school students from Ohio who were suspended without a hearing or an opportunity to present their side of the story. The students and their families filed a lawsuit, arguing that their suspensions violated their constitutional right to due process under the Fourteenth Amendment.

Held: students facing suspensions or expulsions have a constitutional right to due process. The Court recognized that education is of vital importance and that the loss of education due to disciplinary actions can have a significant impact on a student's future. A student facing a suspension of 10 days or less must be given notice of the charges against them and an opportunity to present their version of the events before the suspension takes effect. The Court also emphasized that the student's right to due process includes the right to a hearing, although it need not be a formal or adversarial hearing. Student's right to due process includes the right to know the evidence against them, to confront witnesses, and to have a decision based on evidence presented during the hearing.

Memorization Mnemonics: SS HD (Significant Suspension, Hearing Required). Kid in detention, playing hangman, waiting for a hearing about his suspension from school.

Exam Insight: Due process generally requires notice and hearing, the opportunity to make one's statement, & to call and examine witnesses. When discussing the constitutional limit on public school punishments, explain that significant suspensions or more severe punishments generally require a hearing to ensure due process rights are upheld. Analyze the specific factors and tests established in relevant case law, such as the "minimum due process" standard discussed in Goss v. Lopez, when assessing the constitutionality of disciplinary actions in public schools. Remember to consider the balance between the school's authority to maintain discipline and the students' rights to procedural fairness when evaluating the constitutionality of punishments in the educational context.

Would prohibiting religious groups from meeting on school property violate the Constitution?

Answer: Yes, prohibiting religious groups from meeting on school property would violate the Constitution, specifically the First Amendment's protection of freedom of speech. The Supreme Court has held that public entities, such as schools, must not discriminate against religious speech or treat religious groups less favorably than non-religious groups when it comes to access to public facilities. Of course, such activities would be extra-curricular, attendance could not be mandatory, nor could the extra curricular religious activity however organized be an influence on students' curricular activities and grading.

Relevant Case Citation: Good News Club v. Milford Central School, 533 U.S. 98 (2001). Issue: religious speech & equal access to public schools. Evangelical Christian organization, sought to hold after-school meetings at a public school in Milford Central School District, New York. School district denied the club's request, citing a policy that prohibited the use of school facilities for religious purposes. The Good News Club sued the school district, claiming that the denial violated their First Amendment rights to free speech and free exercise of religion. The Supreme Court ruled in favor of the Good News Club, holding that the school district's denial of access to the club violated the First Amendment. The Court reasoned that the school's policy was based on the content of the club's speech, which was viewpoint discrimination and violated the principle of free speech. The Court further held that the school district's argument that the club's activities would violate the Establishment Clause of the First Amendment was unfounded. It clarified that allowing the club access to school facilities did not constitute the endorsement of religion by the school district.

Memorization Mnemonic: FreeD, freelignation. Freedom of Religion, Discrimination.

Exam Insight: When discussing religious groups meeting on school property, explain that such a the conflict between the First Amendment's protection of freedom of speech, the freedom of religion, and the separation of Church and State. Analyze the specific factors and tests established in relevant case law, such as the "viewpoint discrimination" analysis applied in Good News Club, when assessing the constitutionality of restrictions on religious speech in public settings. Remember to consider the balance between preserving the separation of church and state while respecting individuals' rights to freely exercise their religion when evaluating the constitutionality of restrictions on religious groups' access to public facilities.

When Do citizens have standing to sue the federal or state government, to compel it to act constitutionally?

Answer: Citizens generally do not have standing to sue the government with a general complaint that the government is not acting constitutionally. Standing requires a concrete and particularized injury, directly traceable to the government's actions, and a likelihood that a favorable court decision would redress the injury. A general complaint about the government's overall constitutional conduct is unlikely to satisfy these standing requirements. To satisfy the case and controversy clause complainants must allege a specific particularized injury to their individual legal rights, which could be remedied by court action.

Relevant Case Citation: Lujan v. Defenders of Wildlife, 504 U.S. 555 (1992). Challenge to a federal regulation issued by the Secretary of the Interior, which interpreted a provision of the Endangered Species Act (ESA). The regulation stated that federal agencies need not consider the potential harm to foreign species when undertaking actions outside the United States. Defenders of Wildlife, an environmental organization, filed a lawsuit arguing that the regulation was unlawful. Government argued that the organization lacked standing to sue because it had not suffered a concrete injury. Supreme Court ruled in favor of the government, holding that the Defenders of Wildlife did not have standing to bring the lawsuit. **To establish standing, an organization or individual must show an actual or imminent injury that is concrete and particularized, not hypothetical or speculative.** The Court further clarified that the alleged injury must be fairly traceable to the defendant's conduct and that a favorable court decision must be likely to redress the injury. Defenders of Wildlife failed to demonstrate that their members had suffered a concrete injury. The Court concluded that the organization's alleged injury, which was based on the potential harm to foreign species, was too speculative and remote to establish standing.

Memorization Mnemonic: SIP (Standing, Injury, Redressability)

Exam Insight: Standing, injury in fact, is a prerequisite to any constitutional claim because of the constitutions "case or controversy" clause. This is also why advisory opinions are prohibited. Understanding the requirements for standing to sue are important because the issue recurs in any constitutional law claim! To remember this concept, use the mnemonic SIR (Standing, Injury in fact, Redressable), and think of a man in a suit who discovered his injury in fact has forced him to re-dress. Familiarize yourself with cases like Lujan v. Defenders of Wildlife to gain insight into the relevant legal principles. When discussing the citizen's ability to sue the government for general complaints of constitutional violations, explain that standing requires a concrete and particularized injury, a direct link between the injury and the government's actions, and a likelihood that a favorable court decision would provide redress for the injury. Analyze the specific factors and tests established in relevant case law, such as the three elements of standing discussed in Lujan, when assessing the question of citizen standing to challenge government actions. Remember to emphasize that a general complaint about the government's overall constitutional conduct is unlikely to satisfy the standing requirements, as standing requires a specific injury that can, moreover, be remedied by the court, e.g. some equitable writ notably mandamus, quo warranto.

When may a citizen sue the government to act constitutionally?

Answer:

A citizen may sue the government to act constitutionally when they are individually harmed by an unconstitutional act committed by the state. In order to have standing to sue, the citizen must demonstrate a concrete and particularized injury that is directly caused by the government's unconstitutional conduct. It is insufficient to bring a general harm claim on behalf of all citizens; the harm must be specific to the individual bringing the lawsuit. They must also prove the injury can be remedied by some court order.

Relevant Case Citation: Massachusetts v. EPA, 549 U.S. 497 (2007). Issue: Whether the Environmental Protection Agency (EPA) had the authority to regulate greenhouse gas emissions from motor vehicles under the Clean Air Act. Massachusetts, along with several other states, environmental organizations, and cities, filed a lawsuit against the EPA, arguing that it had a duty under the Clean Air Act to regulate greenhouse gas emissions from motor vehicles. They claimed that the EPA's failure to do so was arbitrary and capricious and violated the Act. Held: EPA had the authority to regulate greenhouse gas emissions from motor vehicles. The Court interpreted the Clean Air Act, specifically the definition of "air pollutant," to include greenhouse gases. The Court found that carbon dioxide and other greenhouse gases are air pollutants that contribute to climate change and pose a threat to public health and welfare. It determined that the EPA had the responsibility to regulate these emissions unless it could provide a reasoned explanation for its decision not to do so. The Court rejected the EPA's argument that it lacked authority to regulate greenhouse gases from motor vehicles because such regulation would be ineffective to address the global issue of climate change. The Court held that the EPA's statutory authority was not dependent on the scope or effectiveness of its regulatory efforts.

Exam Insight: When discussing citizen lawsuits against the government to enforce constitutional obligations, explain that standing requires a concrete and particularized injury that is directly caused by the government's unconstitutional conduct. Analyze the specific factors and tests established in relevant case law, such as the injury-in-fact requirement discussed in Massachusetts v. EPA, when assessing the citizen's standing to challenge government actions. Remember to emphasize that a general harm claim on behalf of all citizens is insufficient; the citizen must demonstrate a specific harm that they have suffered as a result of the government's unconstitutional act. What specific facts make this an actual injury to the plaintiff, as opposed to a generalized injury shared by the public at large? Link specific facts in the exam question to the claimed injury "he is injured *BECAUSE*". Just like algebra you must "show your work"!

Define: Preemption

In U.S. constitutional law, the doctrine of preemption is the principle that federal law can override or preempt state law when there is a conflict between the two. Preemption is based on the Supremacy Clause of the United States Constitution, which states that the Constitution, federal laws, and treaties are the supreme law of the land. Preemption is rooted in the idea that the federal government has the ultimate authority to regulate certain areas of law to promote uniformity and avoid conflicting regulations among the states. There are two main types of preemption: express preemption and implied preemption. When a federal law explicitly states that it preempts state law, it is known as express preemption. Express preemption occurs when a federal law explicitly states that it preempts state law. However, even in the absence of explicit language, federal law can still preempt state law if there is an inherent conflict or if the federal government has occupied the field of regulation. That is implied preemption, which occurs when federal law is so comprehensive or occupies the entire field that it leaves no room for state regulation, or when there is a conflict between federal and state law that cannot be reconciled.

The Supreme Court has recognized several different forms of implied preemption. These include conflict preemption, where it is impossible to comply with both federal and state law simultaneously; field preemption, where federal regulation is so pervasive that it occupies the entire regulatory field; and obstacle preemption, where state law poses an obstacle to the objectives and purposes of federal law.

Preemption arises out of the idea that in a conflict between a federal and state law in an area of concurrent federal and state competence the federal law is supreme (supremacy clause). There are instances where both federal and state laws can coexist and regulate the same area without conflict. Additionally, preemption can be a complex and contentious issue, and courts often have to interpret and balance competing federal and state interests to determine whether preemption applies in a particular case.

Preemption: What factors are considered when determining whether federal law preempts a state law?

Answer: Several factors are considered when determining whether federal law preempts a state law:

1) Whether the matter is traditionally a matter of state or local concern. 2) Whether the state law is consistent with and/or supplements the federal law. 3) Whether compliance with both the federal and state law is simultaneously possible, or whether the regulations are mutually exclusive.

These factors help analyze the relationship between federal and state law and determine whether the federal law displaces or overrides the state law based on the principles of federal preemption.

Relevant Case Citation: Arizona v. United States, 567 U.S. 387 (2012). Immigration enforcement and the authority of states to enact their own immigration laws. Facts: Challenge to Arizona's immigration law. The law contained provisions that required state law enforcement officers to determine the immigration status of individuals they lawfully stopped or detained if there was a reasonable suspicion that the individuals were in the country illegally. It also criminalized certain immigration-related offenses. The federal government, represented by the United States, filed a lawsuit arguing that Arizona's law was preempted by federal immigration laws and regulations. The case reached the Supreme Court to determine the constitutionality of the Arizona law. In a majority decision, the Supreme Court ruled in favor of the federal government, holding that several provisions of Arizona's law were preempted by federal immigration law. Immigration law is federal. The federal government has plenary power over immigration matters. State laws cannot interfere with or undermine the federal government's enforcement priorities and policies. The Court held that Arizona's provision requiring state law enforcement officers to determine the immigration status of individuals during routine stops or detentions was preempted. It determined that the federal government's comprehensive framework for immigration regulation impliedly preempted state efforts to create their own immigration enforcement schemes. The Court upheld one provision of the Arizona law, which allowed state law enforcement officers to inquire about an individual's immigration status during the course of a lawful stop, detention, or arrest if there was reasonable suspicion of unlawful presence. The Court concluded that this provision did not conflict with federal law and did not impose a significant burden on federal immigration priorities.

Memorization Mnemonic: Factors For Preemption: Traditional Local Laws Consistent & Complementary (TLC) or Instead are Inconsistent and Incompatible (II). Compliance with Both Federal and State Law is Im/Possible. (CBI) TLC II CB I

Exam Insight: Understanding the factors involved in determining federal preemption of state law is impotant because whether and how far there is an implied preemption is ever uncertain and thus likely to be essay tested. When discussing federal preemption, explain that the courts examine whether the matter at hand is traditionally within the purview of state or local concern, whether the state law is consistent with or supplements the federal law, and whether compliance with both federal and state law is simultaneously possible. Analyze the specific factors and tests established in relevant case law, such as the "field preemption" and "conflict preemption" analyses discussed in Arizona v. United States, when assessing the question of federal preemption. Remember to consider the balance between federal and state authority and the supremacy of federal law when evaluating the impact of federal preemption on state laws.

Does the presence of a provision within a state law that attempts to resolve conflicts with federal law affect the determination of whether the state law is preempted by federal law?

Answer: No, the presence of a provision within a state law that attempts to resolve conflicts with federal law does not affect the determination of whether the state law is preempted by federal law. Preemption arises out of the supremacy of federal law in areas where there is a conflict between federal and state law. While a State law can be enacted which makes subsequent preemption less likely thanks to careful draftsmanship once there is a preemption the State can do nothing, though the Federation might be convinced to amend the federal law which somehow preempts state law.

Analysis of federal preemption focuses on factors such as the subject matter, consistency with federal law, and the possibility of simultaneous compliance with both federal and state law. A conflict resolution provision within the state law itself is not a direct factor in the determination of preemption.

Exam Tip: While it is important to understand the factors that are considered in determining federal preemption, the presence of a conflict resolution provision within a state law does not play a direct role in the analysis ex post. When discussing the determination of preemption, focus on the relevant factors established in case law, such as the subject matter, consistency with federal law, and the possibility of simultaneous compliance. Remember to analyze the specific factors and tests applied by the courts in relevant cases to assess whether federal law preempts state law.

What happens if the Supreme Court of the United States (SCOTUS) is deciding on a state court ruling and there is a split decision, with a 50% versus 50% outcome?

Answer: In the event of a split decision (50% versus 50%) by the Supreme Court of the United States (SCOTUS) when deciding on a state court ruling, the decision of the highest court that ruled on the matter is affirmed. This outcome is typically referred to as a "per curiam decision," which means that the court's decision is issued collectively by the court as a whole, rather than being attributed to any individual justice.

Exam Tip: Understanding the potential outcomes in the event of a split decision by the Supreme Court is important for constitutional law exams. While it is uncommon for the Supreme Court to issue a split decision, if it does occur, the decision of the highest court that ruled on the matter is affirmed. This principle ensures that there is a clear resolution and finality to the case. Remember to familiarize yourself with relevant case law and analyze the specific circumstances and legal principles involved in split decisions to provide a comprehensive answer.

Discuss the most important cases on preemption law.

Answer: There have been several leading preemption cases in U.S. constitutional law that have shaped the doctrine of preemption. Here are a few notable examples:

1. McCulloch v. Maryland, 17 U.S. (4 Wheat.) 316 (1819): This Supreme Court case established the principle of federal supremacy. The Court held that states cannot tax federal institutions, such as the Second Bank of the United States, because "the power to tax involves the power to destroy." Although not directly addressing preemption, this case laid the foundation for the later development of the preemption doctrine.

2. Gibbons v. Ogden, 22 U.S. (9 Wheat.) 1 (1824): This case involved a dispute over a steamboat monopoly granted by the state of New York. The Supreme Court held that Congress's power to regulate interstate commerce under the Commerce Clause of the Constitution is exclusive and supersedes state laws that interfere with or regulate interstate commerce. It established the principle that federal regulation in areas of exclusive federal authority preempts state regulation.

3. Pennsylvania v. Nelson, 350 U.S. 497 (1956): In this case, the Supreme Court addressed the issue of whether state law could criminalize the act of being a member of the Communist Party. The Court held that federal law, specifically the Smith Act, which regulated the membership and activities of certain organizations, preempts state laws that seek to regulate the same conduct. It emphasized that federal preemption can occur even in the absence of an express provision in federal law.

4. Arizona v. United States, 567 U.S. 387 (2012): This case involved a challenge to an Arizona law, known as SB 1070, which sought to

enforce immigration regulations in a manner that went beyond federal immigration law. The Supreme Court held that several provisions of the Arizona law were preempted by federal immigration law because they interfered with the federal government's authority to regulate immigration policy. The Court reiterated that immigration policy is an area of significant federal authority, and states cannot enact laws that conflict with or frustrate federal objectives.

5. Wyeth v. Levine, 555 U.S. 555 (2009): This case dealt with a conflict between federal regulations regarding prescription drug labels and a state law tort claim against a pharmaceutical company. The Supreme Court held that the federal regulations did not preempt the state law claim because the regulations did not explicitly or implicitly prevent the drug manufacturer from providing additional warnings about the risks associated with the drug. The decision emphasized that federal preemption should not be presumed and that there must be a clear and manifest intent from Congress to preempt state law.

These cases represent significant milestones in the development of the doctrine of preemption, establishing principles that guide the interpretation of conflicts between federal and state laws. Preemption cases are highly fact-specific, and the outcome can vary depending on the specific legal and factual circumstances of each case.

Is it permissible for a state to require a federal worker, who is driving through the state on federal business, to possess a valid state driver's license?

Answer: No, this is obviously unconstitutional for a variety of reasons. First, the U.S. constitution imposes a legal duty on the States to grant full faith and credit to each others' acts. Thus, a driver's license good in one state is, unless there are some special circumstances, valid in other states. Moroever, there is the right to travel, which is protected by the privileges and immunities clause, this law impinges that right. Finally and most relevantly there is the supremacy clause. It is not permissible for a state to require a federal worker, who is driving through the state on federal business, to possess a valid state driver's license. This is due to the Supremacy Clause of the United States Constitution, which establishes that federal law takes precedence over conflicting state laws. Since the federal worker is engaged in official federal business, the state's requirement for a state driver's license would be preempted by federal law.

Relevant Case Citation: McCulloch v. Maryland, 17 U.S. 316 (1819)

Exam Tip: Understanding the Supremacy Clause and federal preemption is essential for constitutional law exams. Remember that the Supremacy Clause establishes the principle that federal law is supreme over state law in cases of conflict. When discussing the permissibility of a state requiring a federal worker to possess a state driver's license, emphasize that the Supremacy Clause precludes such a requirement because federal law takes precedence. Support your answer with relevant case law, such as McCulloch v. Maryland, to demonstrate the historical basis for the Supremacy Clause. Analyze the specific legal principles and factors involved to provide a comprehensive response.

If a local town library is sued for purportedly violating a federal law, can it claim sovereign immunity?

Answer: No, a local town library cannot claim sovereign immunity. The Eleventh Amendment of the United States Constitution does not grant sovereign immunity to localities, cities, counties, towns, or local libraries. Sovereign immunity generally applies to states, protecting them from being sued in certain circumstances, but it does not extend to local government entities such as town libraries. The law generally distinguishes a State's sovereign legal acts (acto iuri imperii), which are immune from private lawsuit, from the state's economic acts (acto iuri gestionis). The sovereign acting as a manager generally does not enjoy immunity. Since the library functions are not governmental (forming, adjudicating, and enforcing law) but are economical acts they ought not enjoy sovereignty.

Exam Tip: The Eleventh Amendment grants sovereign immunity to states, but it does not extend to local government entities. When discussing the ability of a local town library to claim sovereign immunity, explain that local libraries, even when part of a local government as opposed to being a private charity, are not shielded by sovereign immunity from suits in federal court. Emphasize the distinction between state and local government entities when analyzing the application of sovereign immunity. Support your answer with relevant legal principles and doctrines to provide a well-rounded response.

Is it constitutional for a homeowners association (HOA) to pass a rule prohibiting residents from raising the American flag on the 4th of July?

Answer: Yes, it is constitutional for a homeowners association (HOA) to pass a rule prohibiting residents from raising the American flag on the 4th of July. The reason is that the actions of an HOA are generally considered private, and the First Amendment's freedom of speech protections only apply to state actions. State action is required to implicate the First Amendment's freedom of speech, and the actions of a private HOA do not meet the threshold of state action.

Relevant Case Citation: Shelley v. Kraemer, 334 U.S. 1 (1948). Racial restrictive covenants and their (non) enforceability in property agreements. Property dispute in St. Louis, Missouri, where an African American family, the Shelleys, purchased a home in a neighborhood that had a racially restrictive covenant. The covenant prohibited the sale or occupancy of the property by African Americans. When the Shelleys attempted to move into their new home, several neighbors filed a lawsuit seeking to enforce the racially restrictive covenant. Supreme Court ruled in favor of the Shelleys, holding that the enforcement of racially restrictive covenants by state courts was unconstitutional. The Court held that state judicial enforcement of such covenants violated the Fourteenth Amendment's Equal Protection Clause. Racist covenants are private agreements but restrict alienation of property (disfavored at common law) and their enforcement in court would violate the equal protection clauses of the U.S. Constitution. Seeking public enforcement of private law rights can thereby apply the public law constitutional provisions to private law relations.

Exam Tip: Understanding state action is key because in principle the constitution only addresses and state action. Regulation of private law rights and persons is exceptional, though of course there are now

Constitutional Law Quiz Questions & Explanatory Answers, Vol. II

many exceptions thanks to the bill of rights. Nonetheless, state action is usually a threshold issue in almost any constitutional law claim. When discussing the constitutionality of an HOA passing a rule restricting the display of the American flag, explain that the First Amendment's freedom of speech protections generally apply to state actions, not private actions. Emphasize that state action is required to trigger constitutional scrutiny under the First Amendment. Support your answer with relevant case law, such as Shelley v. Kraemer, to demonstrate the importance of state action in constitutional analysis. Analyze the specific legal principles and factors involved to provide a comprehensive response.

Give the Holding in Shelly v. Kramer

Answer: Shelley v. Kraemer, <u>334 U.S. 1</u> (1948), was a landmark United States Supreme Court case that dealt with racial discrimination in housing contracts. The case involved a restrictive covenant that prohibited the sale of property to African Americans in certain neighborhoods.

The plaintiffs, Shelley and other African American buyers, entered into contracts to purchase homes in a racially-restricted neighborhood. The defendants, the Kraemers and other property owners, sought to enforce the restrictive covenant to prevent the sale of the property to African Americans. The restrictive covenant was a private agreement among property owners, but the plaintiffs argued that its enforcement by state courts violated their rights under the Fourteenth Amendment's Equal Protection Clause.

The Supreme Court unanimously held that the enforcement of racially restrictive covenants by state courts was unconstitutional. The Court reasoned that state action, through the judicial system, was involved in enforcing the discriminatory agreements, and thus violated the Equal Protection Clause. It held that the state courts' enforcement of such covenants constituted state-sanctioned racial discrimination.

The decision in Shelley v. Kraemer was significant because it struck down the enforcement of racially restrictive covenants, which were prevalent in housing contracts at the time. The Court's ruling played a role in dismantling the legal framework that supported racial segregation in housing. It emphasized that private agreements that perpetuated racial discrimination could not be enforced by the state without violating the Constitution.

Shelley v. Kraemer contributed significantly to the broader effort to combat racial discrimination and promote equal rights under the law.

It underscored the Court's commitment to eradicating racial segregation and advancing equal protection principles in housing and other areas of public life. It is justifiable from the common law perspective that common law disfavors restrains on alienation.

Define: bill of attainder?

Answer: A bill of attainder is a legislative act that imposes punishment on an individual or a group without the benefit of a proper trial. It is a direct action by the legislative branch to single out and punish specific individuals or groups without the involvement of the judicial branch. Bills of attainder are unconstitutional. The constitutional provision that outlaws bills of attainder and ex post facto laws is found in Article I, Section 9, Clause 3 of the United States Constitution. It states: "No Bill of Attainder or ex post facto Law shall be passed." This clause serves as a safeguard against legislative abuses of power by prohibiting the passage of laws that inflict punishment without judicial trial (bills of attainder) or retroactively criminalize or increase the punishments for past actions (ex post facto laws).

Relevant Case Citation: U.S. v. Lovett, 328 U.S. 303 (1946). Congress passed the "Loyalty Act" which barred certain federal employees deemed disloyal or subversive from receiving salaries or compensation. Three employees, Lovett, Schneiderman, and Brothman, who were affected by the law, filed a lawsuit challenging its constitutionality. Held: Loyalty Act violated the Constitution's Separation of Powers principle. The Court concluded that the law constituted an impermissible legislative intrusion into the executive branch's authority to make personnel decisions. Congress could not single out specific individuals or groups for punishment or disqualification from employment without due process (notice and opportunity for a hearing). Such legislation violated the fundamental principles of fairness and the separation of powers enshrined in the Constitution.

Exam Tip: Understanding the concept of a bill of attainder is important for constitutional law exams. A bill of attainder is a legislative act that declares a person or a group of people guilty of a crime and imposes punishment without the benefit of a trial. Under the United States Constitution, specifically Article I, Section 9, Clause 3, Congress is explicitly prohibited from passing bills of attainder. This prohibition is intended to safeguard individual rights and prevent the government from arbitrarily singling out and punishing individuals or groups. Bills of attainder were historically used in England to target political enemies or individuals deemed threats to the monarchy. The framers of the U.S. Constitution sought to prevent such abuses by including the prohibition on bills of attainder. By prohibiting bills of attainder, the Constitution ensures that individuals are afforded fundamental rights, such as the presumption of innocence, the right to a fair trial, and the opportunity to present a defense. Bills of attainder are expressly considered unconstitutional on both the state and federal levels. When discussing a bill of attainder, explain that it violates the constitutional principle of due process and the separation of powers by bypassing the judiciary and imposing punishment directly through legislative action. Support your answer with relevant case law, such as U.S. v. Lovett, to illustrate the unconstitutionality of bills of attainder. Analyze the specific legal principles and factors involved to provide a comprehensive response.

When a ratified treaty conflicts with an act of Congress, which one takes precedence? Is the rule the same for unratified treaties?

Answer: When a ratified treaty conflicts with an act of Congress, the general rule is that the more recent enactment prevails. This principle, often referred to as the "Last in Time" rule, dictates that the most recently adopted law between the treaty and the act of Congress takes precedence in the event of a conflict. However, an unratified treaty is not domestic law, it has no binding domestic force before U.S. courts. The U.S. executive may however invoke and apply the treaty as evidence of domestic law or as a reflection of binding customary international law. Customary international law is binding in U.S. domestic law, but may be "displaced" by ordinary congressional legislation. That is, in a conflict between the international customary law and ordinary federal legislation or the U.S. constitution the written domestic law prevails over the unwritten international law. In a purported conflict between State legislation and an international customary law the State court would "ignore" the international custom. The adressees of international law are international legal persons. The USA is one, the several states are not. In a conflict between an unratified treaty and a State law the treaty might better prevail because of the exclusive federal foreign policy competence and/or because of the supremacy of federal law, for the unratified treaty is law, but it is not yet directly enforceable. It may be persuasive and indirectly enforceable as in the case of a conflict between a state law, which violates the exclusive foreign policy prerogative of the federation.

Relevant Case Citation: Reid v. Covert, 354 U.S. 1 (1957). International treaties and the rights of U.S. citizens. Spouses of U.S. servicemen stationed overseas charged with the murder of their husbands. The servicewomen were tried and convicted by a military tribunal under the authority of the Status of Forces Agreement (SOFA), an international treaty between the United States and the host country. Tribunal's jurisdiction over U.S. citizens violated the Fifth and Sixth Amendments of the U.S. Constitution. The Court declared that American citizens, whether civilian or military, are entitled to the full protection of the Constitution, regardless of their location or the existence of a treaty. US Constitution is the supreme law of the land, no treaty can supersede its protections and guarantees. It held that the rights guaranteed by the Constitution cannot be diminished or abrogated by international agreements alone. Furthermore, the Court rejected the argument that the SOFA gave the military jurisdiction over the defendants. It concluded that the Constitution's protections for due process and the right to a fair trial could not be overridden by a treaty provision.

Memorization Mnemonic: LIT (Last in Time)

Exam Tip: Understanding the hierarchy between treaties and acts of Congress is essential for constitutional law exams. Remember that the Last in Time rule governs the resolution of conflicts between a ratified treaty and an act of Congress. When discussing the precedence between a ratified treaty and an act of Congress, emphasize that the more recent enactment prevails. Support your answer with relevant case law, such as Reid v. Covert, to demonstrate the application of the Last in Time rule. Analyze the specific legal principles and factors involved to provide a comprehensive response. For bonus points distinguish the case of the unratified treaty or executive agreement, which if they have any binding effect domestically at all could only bind the executive as a political and not legal act.

What is the definition of an at-large election?

Answer: An at-large election is a voting system in which candidates are elected to represent an entire jurisdiction, such as a city or county, rather than being elected from specific geographic districts within that jurisdiction. In an at-large election, voters have the opportunity to cast their votes for candidates across the entire jurisdiction, and the candidates who receive the highest number of votes win the seats available.

Exam Tip: When defining an at-large election, emphasize that it involves the election of representatives for an entire jurisdiction, rather than specific districts within that jurisdiction. Illustrate the voting process in an at-large election, where voters can cast ballots for candidates across the entire jurisdiction. Support your answer with relevant legal principles and doctrines to provide a comprehensive response.

Under what circumstances is an at-large election considered unconstitutional?

Answer: An at-large election is considered unconstitutional when the at-large scheme has the effect of preventing a significant minority from electing any representatives. In such cases, the at-large election system can be deemed discriminatory and in violation of the Equal Protection Clause of the Fourteenth Amendment.

Keywords: discrete and insular politically unpopular minorities with a history of disenfranchisement

Relevant Case Citation: Thornburg v. Gingles, 478 U.S. 30 (1986). Voting Rights Act of 1965. Challenge to the redistricting plan in North Carolina. Allegation: "diluting" the voting strength of African American voters. Plaintiffs argued that the redistricting plan violated Section 2 of the Voting Rights Act, which prohibits any voting practice or procedure that results in the denial or abridgment of the right to vote on the basis of race or color.
1. The minority group must be able to demonstrate that it is sufficiently large and geographically compact to constitute a majority in a single-member district.

2. Minority Group Political Cohesion: The minority group must show that its members vote cohesively, meaning they tend to vote for the same candidates or share common political interests.

3. White Bloc Voting: The white majority must usually vote as a bloc to defeat the preferred candidates of the minority group.

The Court held that if these three elements are established, it could indicate the existence of racially polarized voting and a violation of the Voting Rights Act.

Exam Tip: Understanding the constitutional implications of at-large elections is important for constitutional law exams. Highlight that an at-large election can be deemed unconstitutional if it results in the dilution or exclusion of the voting rights of a substantial minority. When discussing the circumstances in which an at-large election is considered unconstitutional, emphasize the violation of the Equal Protection Clause. Support your answer with relevant case law, such as Thornburg v. Gingles, to illustrate the legal standards used to assess the constitutionality of at-large election schemes. Analyze the specific legal principles and factors involved to provide a comprehensive response.

What is the purpose of the equal protection clause in the Constitution, and how does it safeguard against discriminatory treatment by state governments?

Answer: The equal protection clause of the Constitution serves the purpose of ensuring that state governments do not engage in unjustifiable discrimination by treating individuals or groups differently based on protected characteristics. It prohibits state actions and laws that infringe upon the fundamental right to equal treatment under the law, regardless of race, gender, religion, or other protected attributes. This constitutional provision acts as a safeguard against arbitrary or discriminatory actions by state governments, promoting fairness and equality.

Under what circumstances does private action qualify as state action, triggering the application of constitutional protections such as the equal protection clause?

Answer: Private action can be considered state action when it meets certain criteria that demonstrate significant involvement or entwinement with the government. There are two main scenarios in which private action may be deemed state action:

a) When a private entity performs a function that is traditionally and exclusively carried out by the government. In such cases, the private entity essentially steps into the shoes of the government, and its actions are considered state action subject to constitutional scrutiny.

b) When the government is substantially intertwined or involved in the private action, such that it can be seen as a joint participant or enabler of the discriminatory conduct. This occurs when the government provides significant support, encouragement, or control over the private action, making it effectively an extension of the government's actions.

Answer: Can you provide an example of private action in which the government's involvement is not significant enough to be considered state action, thus exempting it from constitutional scrutiny?

One example of private action where the government is not sufficiently involved to be considered state action is the issuance of a liquor license to a racist organization. In this case, the act of granting a liquor license to the organization would be deemed a private action, as it does not involve significant government involvement or control.

Furthermore, providing police or fire protection services by the government to private individuals or organizations is also not considered state action for the purpose of the equal protection analysis. These services are generally provided to all individuals and are not indicative of the government endorsing or supporting any particular private action.

The determination of state action is fact-specific and may depend on the specific circumstances of each case. Courts consider various factors, including the extent of government involvement, control, and entwinement with the private action, in making this determination.

One relevant U.S. Supreme Court case that discusses the concept of state action is Shelley v. Kraemer (1948). In this case, the Court held that the enforcement of racially restrictive covenants by state courts, which prohibited the sale of property to African Americans, constituted state action and violated the equal protection clause. The Court emphasized that the state courts' enforcement of these private agreements had the effect of state-sanctioned discrimination, making it a state action subject to constitutional scrutiny.

Reference: Shelley v. Kraemer, 334 U.S. 1 (1948)

An example of private action where the government's involvement may not reach the threshold of state action is the issuance of a liquor license to a privately-owned establishment. In this scenario, the government's role is primarily regulatory, and the act of granting a liquor license does not typically amount to substantial government involvement or control over the private entity's actions. As long as the government's licensing decision adheres to non-discriminatory criteria and does not endorse or facilitate discriminatory practices by the private establishment, it may not be considered state action triggering constitutional scrutiny.

The determination of state action is context-specific and depends on the specific facts and circumstances of each case. Courts consider various factors, such as the extent of government entwinement and control, to evaluate whether private action qualifies as state action for the purposes of constitutional analysis.

The concept of state action is important in determining whether constitutional protections, including the equal protection clause, apply in a particular situation. Generally, the equal protection clause applies to actions taken by the government or government entities. However, there are instances where private actions can be considered state action if the government is significantly involved or intertwined with the private action.

Some Final Exam Tips!

1. Understand the Exam Format: Familiarize yourself with the structure and requirements of the exam. Determine whether the exam will consist of multiple-choice questions, essay questions, or a combination of both. Knowing the format in advance will allow you to allocate your time effectively and tailor your preparation accordingly.

2. Review and Organize your Notes: Take the time to review your class notes, outlines, and any supplementary materials you have gathered throughout your constitutional law studies. Organize the information into coherent themes or topics, making it easier to reference during the exam. Consider creating visual aids, such as flowcharts or diagrams, to help you visualize and comprehend complex concepts.

3. Practice with Past Exams: Locate past exams or sample questions that cover constitutional law topics. This will give you a sense of the types of questions you may encounter and allow you to practice applying legal principles to fact patterns. Take the opportunity to develop a systematic approach to answering questions, focusing on issue spotting, analysis, and concise writing.

4. Master the Art of Issue Spotting: Constitutional law exams often present hypothetical scenarios with multiple legal issues embedded within them. Train yourself to identify these issues by carefully reading the fact patterns, highlighting relevant information, and spotting potential legal arguments. Issue spotting is key to providing comprehensive and well-rounded answers.

5. Analyze and Apply Legal Principles: Once you have identified the

legal issues, develop a clear and structured analysis. State the applicable legal principles, cite relevant cases or statutes, and explain how they relate to the facts at hand. Be thorough in your analysis, considering different perspectives and counterarguments where appropriate.

6. Use IRAC Method: The IRAC (Issue, Rule, Application, Conclusion) method is a widely used framework for structuring essay responses. Begin with a clear identification of the issue, state the relevant legal rules, apply those rules to the facts, and conclude with a concise resolution. This method ensures that your answers are well-organized and easy for the examiner to follow.

7. Practice Time Management: Time is a critical factor in exams. Develop a strategy that allows you to allocate an appropriate amount of time to each question or section. Consider the weightage of each question and prioritize accordingly. If you find yourself running out of time, prioritize completing the essential elements of each answer rather than leaving them unfinished.

8. Be Clear and Concise: In written responses, strive for clarity and conciseness. Use clear and coherent sentences, avoid excessive jargon, and focus on providing direct answers. Remember that examiners may have limited time to review each response. Be concise while still addressing all necessary points.

9. Answer the Question Asked! Law school essays aren't poetry. They are analysis and resolution of specific legal problems. Don't discuss irrelevancies, do reason in a structured organized fashion linking the facts of the case to the specific applicable rules and the justifications for the rules.

10. Practice Mindful Revision: Prioritize quality over quantity when it comes to revision. Instead of passively rereading materials, actively engage with the content. Summarize key concepts in your own words, create flashcards or mnemonic devices to aid

Constitutional Law Quiz Questions & Explanatory Answers, Vol. II

memorization, and engage in discussions with classmates to solidify your understanding.

11. Stay Calm and Confident: Exam stress is common, but it's crucial to manage it effectively. Develop a routine that promotes relaxation and self-care during the exam period. Practice mindfulness techniques, maintain a healthy lifestyle, and get adequate rest. Remember that you have put in the effort and preparation, and trust in your abilities.

12. Follow Exam Instructions! Read the exam instructions carefully and ensure that you understand what is required of you. Pay attention to word limits, specific formatting instructions, and any additional guidance provided. Following instructions demonstrates attention to detail and can contribute to earning valuable points. Answer the question asked!

13. Seek Clarification if Needed: If you encounter ambiguous or unclear instructions or questions, don't hesitate to seek clarification from the examiners or your professors. It's better to address any doubts or uncertainties before the exam rather than making assumptions that may lead to inaccuracies in your answers.

Thorough preparation, strategic thinking, and effective time management are key to success in constitutional law exams. By implementing these tips and maintaining a positive mindset, you can approach your exams with confidence and perform to the best of your abilities. Good luck!

CONCLUSION

Tthe journey of preparing for law school final exams and the bar exam can be challenging, but it is also a rewarding and transformative experience. As you dive deep into the intricate details of constitutional law, immerse yourself in the principles and doctrines that govern our legal system. This quizbook provides a comprehensive understanding of various aspects of constitutional law, and it serves as a valuable resource for law students and bar prep candidates. You get out of it what you put in. So work it!

We read and reread many questions and answers about the establishment clause, burdens of proof, different levels of scrutiny, limitations on commercial speech, equal protection, freedom of speech, procedural due process, federalism, the commerce clause, sovereign immunity, and many other fundamental legal concepts. By actively engaging with these questions and their detailed explanatory answers, you have gained a deeper knowledge and appreciation for the complexities of constitutional law.

Yet, the study of law is not only about memorizing rules or even understanding the reasons for the rules. I'ts also about critically analyzing the legal principles, understanding their historical context, and applying them to real-world scenarios. As you progress in your legal education, strive to develop strong analytical skills, sound reasoning, and the ability to articulate persuasive arguments. These qualities will not only aid you in law school examinations but also in your future legal practice.

It is important to approach the study of law with dedication, discipline, and a growth mindset. Embrace the challenges that come your way, for they are opportunities for growth and improvement. Recognize that mistakes and setbacks are part of the learning process, and use them as stepping stones to enhance your understanding and refine your legal reasoning. "Failure is the mother of success" so don't give up! Keep at it!

As you continue your journey to becoming a competent legal professional, remember the profound impact and responsibility that lies within the practice of law. The knowledge you acquire and the skills you develop will empower you to advocate for justice, protect individual rights, and contribute to the evolution of our legal system.

Above all, maintain a sense of resilience, passion, and integrity. Pursuing a career in law requires unwavering dedication, a commitment to ethics, and a genuine desire to make a positive difference in society. If you feel you are fighting for fairness, justice, and equality you will have a much greater more meaningful legal adventure as you navigate the stormy seas of constitutional law.

Finally, surround yourself with a supportive community of mentors, fellow students, and legal professionals who share your passion for the law. Engage in meaningful discussions, seek guidance when needed, and always remain open to new perspectives. Remember the law is a collaborative endeavor, and through collaboration, we can strive together for better world.

Congratulations on your commitment to learning and your pursuit of excellence in constitutional law. With the knowledge and understanding you have gained from this quizbook, combined with your continued efforts and dedication, you are well on your way to achieving your goals and making a positive impact in the legal profession. Good luck on your exam, you can not only pass but even excel if you just put in the work. May your journey be filled with growth, success, fun, and fulfillment!

In closing, if you enjoyed this book feel free to write me an email eric.engle@yahoo.com or even better write a book review. Book reviews help other readers find interesting books and drive the algorithm. You may also enjoy my free search engines, or free online law dictionaries. Thank you for reading!

ABOUT THE AUTHOR

Insert author bio text here. Insert author bio text here

Made in United States
Cleveland, OH
14 December 2024